W9-DER-303

IN DEFENSE OF MARRIAGE

In Defense of Marriage

ART CAREY

WALKER AND COMPANY
NEW YORK

First published in the United States of America in 1984 by the Walker Publishing Company, Inc.

Published simultaneously in Canada by John Wiley & Sons Canada, Limited, Rexdale, Ontario.

The author is grateful to the following source for permission to reprint copyrighted material: *Esquire* magazine for the excerpt on pages 71–73 from "Looking for a Wife" by Lee Eisenberg. Reprinted with permission from *Esquire* (December 1980). Copyright © 1980 by Lee Eisenberg.

Library of Congress Cataloging in Publication Data

Carey, Art.
In defense of marriage.

Outgrowth of an article written for the Philadelphia inquirer magazine published on Feb. 20, 1983.
Bibliography: p.
1. Marriage—United States. I. Title.
HQ536.C355 1984 306.8'1 83-40408
ISBN: 0-8027-0764-5

Book design by Tom Miller

Printed in the United States of America

10 9 8 7 6 5 4 3 2 1

All because of Tanya

ACKNOWLEDGMENTS

This book grew out of an article I wrote for the *Philadelphia Inquirer Magazine* that was published on February 20, 1983. There wouldn't be a book if there hadn't been a magazine article. And there wouldn't have been a magazine article if it hadn't been for two people: Carolyn White, the former managing editor of the *Inquirer Magazine,* whose enthusiasm and encouragement kept me going during periods of doubt; and David R. Boldt, editor of the *Inquirer Magazine*—and a friend, mentor and trusted advisor—who has always believed in me and who gave me the freedom to explore this important subject with the care and thoroughness it deserves.

The magazine article wouldn't have become a book if it hadn't been for Beth Walker, who saw its promise and communicated her excitement about it to others (including me), and Tom Miller, who, through gentle guidance and deft editing, helped me craft a rather rough-hewn manuscript into the finished book you have before you now.

Finally, there wouldn't have been an author if it hadn't been for my beloved grandfather, Edward A. Lynch, whose principled behavior has always been a shining example of manly character and whose kindness and loyalty to his wife I shall always strive to emulate.

In Defense of Marriage

ONE

"Why Did You Do It?"

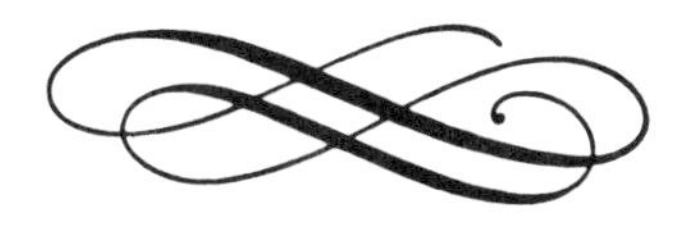

NOT LONG AGO, SHORTLY after I returned from the honeymoon following my second marriage, I was greeted at the office by an older married colleague whom I've come to respect for his professional skills and wisdom about life.

"Hey, Artie, I heard you got married."

"Sure did," I said, beaming.

"You really blew it. You had everything going for you. Why did you do it?"

My face fell. I looked at him again to make sure he wasn't kidding. He wasn't. Nonplussed, I resorted to paraphrasing Samuel Johnson, stammering out, "It's a triumph of hope over experience."

It was not the first time I'd encountered such a response. During the months I was engaged, several friends and acquaintances expressed similar sentiments, though usually not as bluntly. Sometimes they would say something positive and blithe, but all the while they were looking at me in a way that seemed both rueful and disbelieving, as though I'd just told them I was planning to do something heroic, romantic and doomed, like row across the Atlantic in a six-foot dinghy.

To some extent, I'd asked for it. During the time I was single, I'd written an incendiary magazine article about single women that gave some people the impression I was a merry divorcé or bachelor stud. "So how many dates do you have tonight?" friends would kid me in the hallways. One office wag regularly referred to me as "Mr. Single." And when a local newspaper published an interview with me in which I stated I liked marriage and looked forward to marrying again, a jaded colleague said, "You were just kidding, weren't you?"

So perhaps it shouldn't have been surprising that others were surprised when I decided to take the plunge. Nevertheless, their reactions were unnerving. "There's a wild rumor going around that you're getting married," said a bachelor running buddy a few days after I'd announced my engagement. "Can you believe it?" And when I broke the news to a close single friend, she eyed me levelly for several moments and said, "It's so quaint. You rarely hear of people actually *doing* it anymore."

Some of my more macho single male friends simply thought I was crazy. "Your fiancée may be terrific," they seemed to be saying, "but there are all those lovely, hard-charging career women out there—lonely, hungry, willing, able, up for anything! How could you pass it all up?" It was like walking away from a lavish buffet (courtesy of the sexual revolution and the women's movement) with only one meager entree.

This anti-marriage attitude was not universal, but it was prevalent enough to make me wonder. Of course, when you work at a newspaper as I do, you're not working in the real world. Journalism has been called "the last refuge of the perpetual adolescent," and the *Philadelphia Inquirer*, the paper for which I work, is as one friend put it, "a treehouse for delinquent adults." That's one reason it's so much fun. The *Inquirer* is crawling with geniuses and egomaniacs as well as the usual assortment of wackos, weirdos, neurotics and paranoiacs. Now, at a law firm or corporate office, you're liable to find just as many oddballs, but at a newspaper, people are both allowed and encouraged to let it all hang out. Newspapers tend to attract free spirits, people who are vigorously independent and pride themselves on traveling light and being hip, fast-moving and fashionably cynical. To people of such temperament, marriage, naturally enough, often seems stifling and confining.

But the skepticism I sensed toward marriage was not confined to the trendy vagabonds at the *Inquirer.* It seemed as though society in general—or at least its opinion molders and tastemakers—had decided marriage was frumpy and obsolete.

I resented that. I resented the way the media glamorize the nomadic romantic habits of childishly fickle celebrities. Every day, it seems, newspaper gossip columnists are tittering over the latest "loves" of such models of steadfast affection as Warren Beatty and Elizabeth Taylor. Meanwhile, the everyday joys of successful marriages are non-stories. To the fans of prime-time soaps like *Dallas* and *Dynasty,* marriages are interesting only when they are splintering or being violated. In movies such as *Ordinary People* and *Shoot the Moon,* marriage takes its natural course: crumbling, crushing souls, igniting vicious fury. To be married, it seems, is to be boring, bourgeois, stunted, frustrated. It is the end of adventure, the end of precious freedom.

Or so some believe. But not I.

I believe in marriage, and my belief has nothing to do with religion or some idealistic view of human nature. I grew up in an affluent suburb, the Philadelphia Main Line: a Cheeveresque landscape populated by polished, proper gentry who seemed to have everything—gilt pedigrees, ivied educations, sprawling mansions on leafy lanes, Mercedes-Benz station wagons, strong-chinned blond children attending the right prep schools. But so many of these fortunate people seemed unhappy, shackled in disastrous marriages—sham, adulterous marriages that existed solely for social convenience, cold hateful marriages that warped their children's lives and boiled over into scenes right out of *Who's Afraid of Virginia Woolf.*

My parents divorced when I was twelve. They probably never should have married. My mother was only eighteen when she walked down the aisle, a shapely, vivacious blonde with an impish smile and a rebel's spirit. My father was a tall, broad-shouldered macho football hero and life-of-the-party fraternity man. They looked great together, Guy Madison and Marilyn Monroe, but they had no idea who the other was or what they were getting into. The marriage had many problems, and there were, eventually, occasional eruptions of violence: liquor bottles flying across the kitchen or being shattered against the sink; my mother attacking my father, her fists flying; my father wrestling her to the floor, trying to restrain her; the police arriving to quell the fracas, while we children cowered in the corner, weeping in terror.

After her divorce, my mother had several love affairs—some better than others, but none completely satisfying. Then, more out of desperation than anything else, she married a pompous doctor whom no one ever really liked and whose appeal no one could ever understand. There were several broken engagements, then an impetuous Nevada wedding. Within weeks, the marriage came unglued, degenerating into a spectacular orgy of bitterness and recrimination that nudged my mother over the edge. She had a nervous breakdown and was institutionalized for months. She was never the same again.

I relate all this to make it clear that when it comes to marriage I'm no starry-eyed Pollyanna. I realize that marriage is not nirvana, that it's no panacea, and that it's not right for everybody. Some marriages are bloody battlefields of clashing egos, others are spirit-eroding purgatories of thwarted desire and ambition. Sometimes, the kindest thing a person can do for a marriage is to get out—as I did myself a few years ago.

By the time my wife and I decided to get divorced, we had been married more than six years.

We met at a summer resort when we were both about to be juniors in college. Kathy was a riding instructor there—a classy, regal-looking woman whose natural reserve and acute nearsightedness made her seem, to me at least, slightly supercilious and irresistibly unapproachable. I was a gardener—raffish, spunky, brimming with teenage muscularity and boyish insouciance, my long, curly, sun-bleached hair tumbling over the red headband that was then the badge of the weekend radical. We had a lovely summer romance that blossomed into a long-term commuter relationship. We both liked English literature and intelligent movies and we shared the same sense of the ironic and absurd. We got married less than a year after college.

Six years later—on that fall Sunday night when Kathy came to me and told me she had fallen in love with another man and asked me whether I thought our marriage was worth saving, and I said probably not—we still laughed at each other's clever wisecracks and still shared the same East Coast, left-liberal, intellectual-elite view of the world. But the passion was gone, if it had ever really been there. Over the past couple of years, we had been living less and less like a married couple and more like roommates, our increasingly separate interests taking us farther and farther away from each other. In the end, we decided to save our friendship by abandoning our marriage.

Getting divorced was the most painful experience of my life. For me—a person used to winning all the prizes, for whom everything came easily—it was my first major, public failure. At first, I couldn't believe it was really happening. It was not part of my life plan, the way I'd envisioned things unfolding when I was younger. For several weeks, I just felt numb and detached, and it took a great effort just to go through the motions of everyday life. Sometimes, when I tried to relieve the grief by running, my chest would fill up with such a clog of anger, regret and fear that I could no longer breathe, and the strength would drain from my legs so that I'd have to stop and walk. Later, as the finality of the divorce began to register, I affected a hardy cheerfulness and macho nonchalance. But inside, I felt defeated and lonely. During this time, I would often stay at the office until well past midnight because I had no reason to leave. When I finally went home, I would sit in a chair in the living room for hours, just staring at the ceiling. Sometimes, I would fall asleep in my clothes and wake up the next morning feeling so melancholy and weary that I was tempted to call in sick. I was surviving on a diet of peanut butter and cereal because I was too listless to cook and wash dishes. A long-time fitness fanatic, I began neglecting my workouts. Run? Lift weights? Do push-ups? What for? Who cared? My lust for life began to wane; I could see the stress taking its toll on my face, etching furrows in my brow, clouding my hitherto sunny smile.

As I write this, four years have passed since my divorce, and I know that I still haven't completely recovered. Yet, if I were caught in another unhappy marriage, I'd go through it all again. For to me there's nothing worse than a bad marriage—and nothing better than a good one. For all my exposure to unpleasant, unsuccessful marriages, I still believe in the institution.

My belief in marriage stems partly from a respect for tradition. But it also reflects my conviction that marriage has lasted as long as it has because, by and large, it works. For all its many imperfections, it is still the best arrangement people have come up with for structuring relationships, organizing family and kin and, as a married friend of mine put it, "being the best you can be." "Living with someone in a controlled relationship like marriage is what we're supposed to do," an unmarried woman friend said. "It's what we're wired for."

I like the way it was put by Dr. Walter Brackelmanns, a marital therapist who is host of a syndicated television show called *Couples.* In an interview in *Us* magazine, he said: "Marriage is a very imperfect institution full of imperfect people struggling to hide from or resolve problems. It is, however, the only place where two people have a chance at an intimate, warm, caring, loving, meaningful, deep, total and real relationship with each other."

My appreciation for marriage is not new-found. This is no song of repentance by a reformed rake, nor is it a herpes-inspired paean to monogamy by a born-again puritan. When I was single, I was single with gusto, but for me the pleasures of bachelorhood never matched the pleasures of married life. In fact, my experiences during that period, if anything, only affirmed my belief in marriage and fired my longing for its quiet, subtle joys.

This, then, is an unabashed celebration of marriage, a kind of conscientious objection to the ways in which this worthy institution has been attacked, undermined and ridiculed. It is also a salute to those who have the courage, optimism and spirit of adventure to get married, and those who, through energy, stamina, maturity, compassion, determination, wisdom, faith and love, have managed to keep their marriages happy.

TWO

Still Popular After All These Years

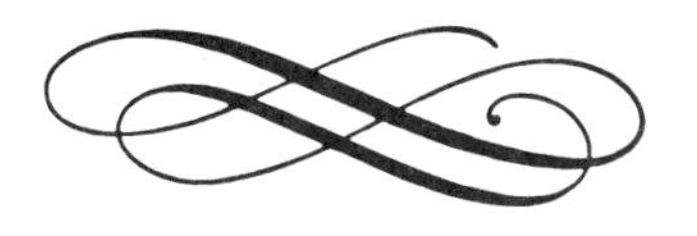

MANY CONFIRMED SINgles who delight in denouncing marriage fancy themselves original thinkers or social radicals. But marriage has always had its critics. "To marry is to halve your rights and double your duties," declared Arthur Schopenhauer, the German philosopher. "Marriage is like life," said Robert Louis Stevenson, ". . . a field of battle, and not a bed of roses." Spanish novelist Miguel de Cervantes called marriage "a noose," and British dramatist William Congreve said that "though marriage makes man and wife one flesh, it leaves 'em still two fools." In a similar vein, American writer Ambrose Bierce defined marriage as "a community consisting of a master, a mistress, and two slaves, making in all, two." And playwright Thornton Wilder claimed that "the best part of married life is the fights. The rest is merely so-so."

For all the nasty gibes, though, marriage until lately was still basically respected, most people agreeing with Menander, the Athenian comedy writer who said, "Marriage, if one will face the truth, is an evil, but a necessary evil."

Then came the sixties: free love, polymorphous perversity and an ethos that exhorted, "If it feels good, do it." Marriage was just one more Establishment institution that impeded "the revolution," another ruling-class instrument of oppression. Suddenly, it was all very serious. As some women shook their fists at Father Nature for cursing them with a womb, feminists such as Kate Millett and Betty Friedan were criticizing marriage for turning women into chattels and twisting their psyches into pretzels. Marriage, charged Millett in *Sexual Politics,* is a tool for perpetuating patriarchal tyranny and confining women "to the cultural level of animal life." Another feminist, Judith Brown, called marriage "an anachronism" that is "oppressive politically, exhausting physically, stereotyped emotionally and sexually, and atrophying intellectually. . . . [It] is the atomization of a sex so as to render it politically powerless."

While most women rejected such extreme views, more and more women, observed Christopher Lasch in *The Culture of Narcissism,* were beginning to regard marriage as "the ultimate trap, the ultimate routine in a routinized society, the ultimate expression of the banality that pervades and suffocates modern life."

Who needed marriage (and husbands) now that women were lugging their own briefcases and cashing their own paychecks? Who needed marriage (and wives) now that practically any man could walk into practically any singles bar on any night of the week and, for the price of a few drinks, go home with a bra-less nymphet who would guide him through the *Kamasutra?* It was the Age of Aquarius, an era of love, peace and happiness, with far-out drugs and no-hassle sex—two popular diversions, Lasch notes, that created "the illusion of intense experience without emotion."

Then came the seventies, and from sea to shining sea, everyone was "into" the Self, which they "actualized" by looking out for Number One, meditating, jogging, Rolfing, esting, Lifespringing, swinging, swapping, marinating in hot tubs, stalking sensation, fleeing from feeling and prostrating before the latest self-help guru or cult prophet. "My heart belongs to me," sang Barbra Streisand. "There is no Mr. Right," proclaimed the brave new single women. "There is Mr. *Right Now.*" Forget marriage, forget the family, forget the future and death. We're all gonna get nuked anyway, so why not boogie into the apocalypse? You only go around once in life, so grab for all the gusto you can get. I do my thing and you do your thing. I gotta do it my way—or no way at all. I need my space. I am my own work of art. The end product is ME!

Marriage, with its demands for sacrifice, compromise and surrender, hardly had a chance.

There was Mom, her consciousness raised, ditching Dad and the kids so she could run off with the twenty-five-year-old Omar Sharif look-alike who was teaching her how to fly. And there was Dad, suddenly growing sideburns, wearing bellbottoms, pumping iron, driving a fire-engine red Corvette, and cavorting with what Tom Wolfe, in his book *In Our Time,* called the "New Cookie"—"the girl in her twenties for whom the American male now *customarily* shucks his wife of two to four decades when the electrolysis gullies appear above her upper lip."

Marriage, it seemed, was fast becoming, as Gore Vidal proclaimed, "no more than a ceremonial vestige of a bygone era." In 1960, when the U.S. population was 179 million, there were 393,000 divorces and the divorce rate was a moderate 2.2 divorces for every 1,000 persons. By 1982, when the national population was 231 million, the number of divorces had more than tripled, to 1,180,000, and the divorce rate had more than doubled, to 5.1 per 1,000, one of the highest rates in the world. In 1973, for the first time in history, divorce ended more marriages than death; by mid-decade, for every two couples marching down the aisle, one couple was clawing its way into court.

Among the children of the baby boom, marriages were even more ephemeral. Since 1960, the divorce rate for couples under 30 has quadrupled. For couples under 25, it has jumped 50 percent in just seven years.

"Previous generations were taught that life is hard, sacrifice is necessary, and unhappiness a cross that sometimes must be borne," explains Landon Y. Jones in *Great Expectations.* "But the baby boomers were not willing to make the risky and often painful compromises their parents did. Just as they had great expectations for themselves, they had great expectations for their marriages. Life was too short to live with an unhappy marriage. If they could switch to another TV channel, why not switch husbands or wives? In fact, their satisfaction and sense of self-obligation practically demanded it."

There were other ominous signs. Eager to prolong their irresponsible adolescence, terrified of surrendering any personal freedom, young people bought condos and shunned matrimony en masse. From 1970 to 1980, the proportion of unmarried women between 25 and 29 doubled, and the number of unmarried couples living together tripled, soaring from 532,000 to 1.5 million. From 1970 to 1983, the number of people living alone leaped 77 percent, to 19.3 million from 10.9 million. And among never-married women, according to two University of Michigan surveys, as reported in Jessie Bernard's *The Future of Marriage,* the feeling that marriage was "all burdens and restrictions" doubled from 36 percent in 1957 to 72 percent in 1976. Watching these trends, some social scientists began wondering whether conventional marriage and the family, the basic unit of cultural transmission, were doomed to extinction.

Then came the eighties, and the signals were mixed.

On the one hand, pop singer Olivia Newton-John, the blonde girl next door turned vamp, was beseeching her audiences to "get physical," and willowy sex surveyor Shere Hite was lamenting the fact that 72 percent of married men had cheated on their wives after only two years. In big cities, some husband-hunting women smoldered because every other good-looking man, it seemed, was gay; among singles, hostility between the sexes was so fierce that some men and women sought refuge in celibacy.

On the West Coast, trendies were pioneering the three-day relationship: love, boredom and rage in one weekend. "You *pretend* to have superficial feelings for me," complains a character in *True Love,* Herbert Gold's novel about contemporary California. "But all you really want is my body and soul and true love." Meanwhile, in New York, the Reverend Sun Myung Moon made a farce of marriage by joining 2,075 couples, most of whom had just met each other, in a mass ceremony in Madison Square Garden.

On the other hand, there were calls, at first timid, then increasingly bold, for an end to promiscuity and a return to romance. Soon, women's magazines were decrying the epidemic of "commitmentphobia" and reminding their baffled "liberated" readers, "You have a right to say no, too." Polls began showing a growing disenchantment with loveless sex; even men were admitting they were bored with bedroom acrobatics and more interested in love and companionship.

Indeed, for all the flirting with alternatives, traditional values and aspirations had apparently held firm. In 1970, 96 percent of all Americans declared themselves dedicated to the ideal of two people sharing a life and a home together. A decade later, the percentage was exactly the same. Furthermore, the marriage rate, after bottoming out in 1976 and 1977, began climbing again. In 1982, there were more marriages—2,495,000—than ever before. At the same time, the divorce rate finally began leveling off.

Awash in nostalgia and a new wave of conservatism, millions of Americans clicked on their television sets to gape at the storybook wedding of Prince Charles and Lady Diana, and, on a less sublime level, the much-ballyhooed nuptials of Luke and Laura on *General Hospital.* Charlie, that bouncy, liberated career girl of the perfume ads, was now pausing to listen to a boyfriend *propose,* and after months of agonizing ambivalence, Rick Redfern of "Doonesbury" finally tied the knot with Joanie Caucus. Moviegoers wept as they witnessed the sunset love of Norman and Ethel Thayer in *On Golden Pond* or watched Richard Gere literally sweep his girlfriend off her feet in the swooning climax of *An Officer and a Gentleman.*

Growing older, many baby boomers began yearning for security and stability. Having too much freedom and too many options was exhausting, they realized, and trying to love in a moral and ethical vacuum was about as exhilarating as hopscotching across a minefield in snowshoes. It was nice to have limits, an acceptable excuse for abstinence, even if, for the time being, it had to be something physical, like herpes, "the new Scarlet Letter," as *Time* dubbed it. While Helen Gurley Brown was still exhorting her *Cosmo* girls to "mouseburger" their way to the ultimate instant orgasm and Hugh Hefner was still peddling the gospel of erotic hedonism, George Leonard, in *Esquire,* that one-time bulwark of Hemingwayesque he-manism, was proclaiming "the end of sex" and singing the praises of "High Monogamy."

At the same time social critic Daniel Yankelovich was heralding a new "ethic of commitment," and sociologists were discovering that despite the *sturm und drang* of the past twenty years, marriage was stronger than ever. "Marriage is far from withering away in contemporary America and is, in fact, enjoying unprecedented popularity," asserted Mary Jo Bane in *Here to Stay*, a book she conceived because she believed marriage was in trouble. "The majority of marriages do not end in divorce. The vast majority of divorced people remarry. Only a tiny proportion of people marry more than twice. We are thus a long way from a society in which marriage is rejected or replaced by a series of short-term liaisons."

Indeed, among the hordes lately rushing to the altar have been many second-timers. Four out of five divorced men and three out of four divorced women are remarrying, usually within three years. "People may have given up on their own marriages, but they have not given up on the institution," says Andrew Cherlin, associate professor of sociology at Johns Hopkins University. "People still seem to need the security and stability that marriage provides."

Today, to an almost universal degree, the United States is still "a marrying society," especially by comparison to the rest of the world, says Paul C. Glick, an Arizona State University sociology professor who was formerly the U.S. Census Bureau's senior demographer. A surprising 95 percent of adult Americans marry at least once during their lifetime, and studies show that married people are generally happier, healthier and more successful than the unmarried. Although many baby boomers are remaining single into their thirties, Glick and others expect the popularity of marriage to slip only a few notches in the future. At some point, roughly nine out of ten Americans will try marriage, and marriage will continue to be the preferred way to live.

"The idea that marriage has become passé is bunk," says University of Pennsylvania sociology professor Frank F. Furstenberg, Jr. "The high rates of divorce in our society indicate not that marriage has been denigrated but that it's been exalted to a point where it seems almost unattainable. There's a tremendous premium on marital gratification now. People feel they have an obligation not to be married unless they're in love, unless the relationship meets their standards for what an ideal marriage should be."

Today, people are dissatisfied with marriage not because it's any worse, but because it's getting better. And the better marriage is, the more people expect from it. Some demand that it be an emotional refuge from the stresses of an impersonal corporate world. Others demand that it provide the comfort and security that religion or community offered in the past. As our lives have become more computerized and secularized, we have become more aware of time, more insistent on fast results and instant gratification. We become impatient when our marriages are not there to succor us, when we discover that our marriages require work, sacrifice and discipline.

Yet, in the final analysis, the alternatives to marriage are not really viable alternatives at all. For all the allure of freedom, most people still prefer the limits of marriage. There is something about marriage that just feels right. It is, after all, a joining in the mind and soul as natural as the joining in the flesh that creates new life. To feel your wife's warm, soft body on a cold winter night, to watch secretly from a window as she tenderly nurtures the flowers in her garden, to think the same thoughts and to feel the same feelings at the very same time, to share moments of deepest recognition without exchanging a word—these are experiences that can only be felt, not described. Nevertheless, they are tokens of the intimacy, the mutuality, the mystic unity that led the church to consider marriage a sacrament, and that guarantee that marriage will survive.

THREE

A Hard Time for Lovers

MONTAIGNE, THE SIXteenth-century French essayist, once compared marriage to a cage: "The birds without despair to get in, and those within despair of getting out."

In the last years of my first marriage, as it became more and more obvious that my wife and I had made a mistake and that our relationship had no future, I began feeling trapped and frustrated. In my travels as a reporter, I occasionally met women who made it clear to me they were available for an affair. I'd always resisted such temptations because of my old-fashioned belief in the sanctity of a vow, and because I knew that my wife would be hurt if she ever found out.

Still, it was tough. My marriage was so moribund and the opportunities for extramarital flings so numerous that sometimes I felt like a sucker. Under the circumstances, was being so honorable really healthy? I began asking myself. Maybe I was just too inhibited, too tyrannized by a vestigial Irish Catholic superego really to live. Soon I began imagining how wonderful it would be to be single. I began envying my single friends their freedom and the variety and excitement of their romantic lives.

After I got divorced and became single again, however, I soon realized that the joys of singlehood were about as substantial as meringue, about as durable as an ice cube in August. What's more, many of the single people I met—far from leading the kind of swinging, no-strings lives depicted in Club Med brochures—were actually lonely, miserable and eager to get married.

But finding a prospective mate isn't easy, they told me, especially if you're a woman. In a nutshell, several female friends complained, all the good men are either married, gay or impotent. And what remains is a depressing Felliniesque collection of nerds, wimps, creeps, goons, brutes, louts, macho superstuds, commitment-loathing cads, rakes, roués, lounge lizards, sexual cowboys, philanderers, recently separated or divorced emotional cripples, hedonists, narcissists, mother-seeking boy-men, puerile preppies, mealy-mouthed liberals, constipated reactionaries, around-the-clock jocks, dimwitted muscleheads, yahoos, peckerwoods, bozos, gun nuts, sleazos, cretins, drunks, dopeheads, space cadets, philistines, cheapskates, ne'er-do-wells, jerks, joggers and other bores.

"Most of the men today want fast results," griped one woman acquaintance. "They want you in bed that night and out the next morning. They tell you they'll call you, but you never hear from them again. Most of us are tired of that scene. There's got to be something more."

Another woman, a divorcée with an eleven-year-old son, told me: "I've been on my own for two years now and I just can't find any good men. The only place you can find them is at work, but if you're trying to be professional, you don't want to get involved with someone on the job. And if you go to a singles bar, you meet two types of guys: the ones who want to get married and are looking for a mother, and the ones who are already married and want to fool around. It's not only hard to find a good man—it's hard to find a date."

The single men I talked to were equally dissatisfied. Women today, they alleged, either don't know what they want from today's man, or else they want far too much. In one breath, women say they want a man who is sensitive and loving; in the next, they dismiss nice guys as wimpy and boring. They talk of a meaningful, long-term relationship—something that will last longer than a night or weekend—or they dream of an idyllic, white-picket-fence future with a kind, nurturing husband, but the man they often lust for is the roguish cad in the Mercedes 380 SL, somebody who reminds them of the dashing Hollywood hunks who've stirred their fantasies since they wore pigtails. One bachelor friend groused, "Women want a man who will hold the car door open for them, who is rich enough to take them to the classiest restaurant in town and vulnerable enough to cry through the whole meal—the perfect date."

In the words of Judy Collins, these are "hard times for lovers." Women are angry at men for being unreliable Casanovas and men are angry at women for being capricious opportunists. After the sexual revolution, the women's movement, gay liberation and the anti-feminist backlash, both sexes, it seems, are confused and frightened: confused about what roles to play and how they should act, frightened about taking an emotional risk in a time when everything is so volatile. As a result, despite their best intentions and best efforts, many young people today who would like to be married have been unable to find someone to be married to.

It's especially tough for women who are attractive, intelligent and well educated. Imbued with the gospel of the women's liberation movement, many of these women graduated from college and professional school believing they could have it all—a career, a man, a family. Professionally, they've achieved success beyond their wildest dreams, but in their relationships with men, they've met with disappointment, misery and failure.

"I consider myself very attractive," a woman lawyer told me recently. "I swim every night. I jog. I play tennis. I read tons of books. I eat yogurt and granola and own my own condo. I have everything except a man. Most of my friends are in the same boat. Every time I get together with another woman, we always end up talking about the Man Question.

"The other day, I went to dinner with five girlfriends from work. All of us are attractive single women in our mid- to late twenties, and only one in five is seeing anybody, and that guy is a bastard who won't marry her. These are just work friends. And then I thought about all my other friends who could just as easily be sitting at that table."

Another single woman, a journalist, said, "I'm in a job where I can meet anyone I want. I'm out all the time, and there's nothing. After a while, you begin to wonder whether it's because there's something wrong with you, whether you're putting out the wrong vibes. I hope to God it's not like this for all professional women.

"In the past year, I've gone out with only two men, both of whom I didn't even like. If I was seventeen, I'd kill myself. It's only because I have really good girlfriends and a really great job that I don't spend a lot more time crying about it. If someone told me that the way it's been for the last two years is the way it's going to be for the rest of my life, I don't think I could take it."

The numbers tell the story: In 1980, in the population as a whole, U.S. Census figures show there were nearly 30 million unmarried women and just 21.5 million unmarried men. Among singles of prime marrying age, those between 25 and 35, women outnumbered men by more than half a million. And of the 19.3 million Americans who were living alone in 1983, only four out of ten were men.

Aggravating the "man shortage" is what sociologists term "the marriage gradient"—the traditional tendency for men to "marry down" and women to "marry up." It is not unusual to see a man in his forties married to a woman in her twenties. And "the older a man gets, the younger he dips down for a wife," says demographer Paul Glick. What this means for a woman in her thirties is that she is competing for a husband not only against her female peers, but also against the new crop of women advancing through their twenties.

Theoretically, such a woman could seek the company of older men, and many do. The hitch, though, is that women now between 25 and 35 were born during the post-World War II baby boom, while the men who might "marry down" to them—men in their forties and fifties—were born during a time when the fertility rate was low. The result: again too many women, not enough men.

Paradoxically, when a woman is smart, well educated and successful, her chances in the marriage market are even worse, for men often marry women who are not only younger but also inferior socially, educationally, intellectually and economically. "Many men feel uncomfortable with a wife who is superior," says Glick. "It's partly because of male chauvinism. The man wants to be Number One in the family, and it's less easy to do that in situations in which the wife is better educated and has a better job."

The sad truth, as I see it, is that most men's egos are as fragile as match sticks. In order to feel like men, most men have to feel important, special, powerful, in charge (why else do you think men are always showing off, building skyscrapers, leading armies, picking fights?). When a woman can do anything a man can, and often do it better (and make babies to boot), she poses a terrible threat. How can a man be lord and master of all he surveys—a role most men, consciously or unconsciously, assume is their natural right, the women's movement notwithstanding—when his wife is smarter or makes more money? How can a man relax from the stresses of the carnivorous corporate world when his wife is competing for power at home? The answer, I'm afraid, is that most men cannot. Instead, they choose mates whose subordinate status makes them feel superior, in control, confident, dominant, virile—like a Man.

So while the best men are marrying down, the best women not only are not marrying up, but in many cases, are not marrying at all. Among women with five or more years of college, for example, nearly 12 percent have never married. By contrast, among all women, only 4.3 percent have never married. "At every age bracket," writes Jessie Bernard in *The Future of Marriage*, "the more income a girl or woman has, the lower the rate of marriage, a situation just the reverse of that of men."

What's left for these "unselected" women is not very appetizing. Ms. Bernard explains: "By and large, both men and women tend to marry mates with the same general class and cultural background; there is 'homogamy.' But within that common background, men tend to marry women slightly below them in such measurable items as age, education and occupation, and presumably in other as yet unmeasurable items as well. The result is that there is no one for the men at the bottom to marry, no one to look up to them. Conversely, there is no one for the women at the top to look up to; there are no men who are superior to them. The result is that the never-married men tend to be 'bottom-of-the-barrel' and the women 'cream-of-the-crop.' " Declares *Savvy* magazine: "The female elite have become demographic losers: They've priced themselves out of the market."

What all of this means for the young single woman—especially the bright, articulate, successful single woman—is that she is living alone. Between 1970 and 1978, the number of women 25 to 34 who had never married rose by more than 111 percent, while the number of women in the same age group who were divorced and not remarried increased by 170 percent. Meanwhile, the number of women 25 to 34 who were married and living with a husband increased by only 17 percent. "It's worse than just a wasteland," one woman told me. "It's a No Man's Land."

From what I saw when I was single, I'd have to agree. At times, I was ashamed for my sex when women told me their horror stories—the seemingly sensitive man who talked of love and feminism until he "scored," and then never called again; the cheat who swept a woman off her feet until she called his home by accident and discovered he was married; the domineering doctor who pretended to be separated and monogamous but who was sleeping with several women at once, including his wife. Sometimes, these men were my friends—wonderful, decent chaps to go biking or canoeing with, to discuss life and the big questions with —but in their relationships with women, perfect rats. They admitted it too, sometimes even boasted about it, their tone of voice hostile, as though they were retaliating against women for being so uppity, so aggressive, so insufferably *liberated.*

And yet, how could men possibly be angry? I wondered. From what I can see, the young single man today is sitting in the proverbial catbird seat. Indeed, for the energetic, good-looking, successful bachelor, the world is an abundant smorgasbord of wonderful women, and many men in such circumstances are, as one woman put it, "living like Warren Beatty." "There are so many women willing to give sex these days that a lot of guys figure, Why bother to get married?" says Dr. David Reed, a suburban Philadelphia psychotherapist. "In the past, dating led to mating; today, dating has become an end in itself."

Because there are so many single adults today, the social pressure to get married is no longer as great as it once was. "It used to be that a man had to get married, found a family and be a breadwinner to prove his masculinity," says Dr. Reed. "If a man didn't get married, he was considered gay. Likewise, a woman who didn't get married was considered an old maid. Today, living alone is being accepted by society."

No longer compelled to conform to the breadwinner ethic, many young men today have regressed. They have become boring, selfish Peter Pans, lacking character, spine and a sense of responsibility. Their idea of an interesting conversation is bragging about their credentials, their latest coups in the courtroom or boardroom, their heroics in last weekend's softball or touch football game. "They have no depth and all they want to do is play," griped a single woman friend. "I want to talk about relationships, feelings, life, and things that mean a lot, and the men want to go out and throw the volleyball around."

Another single woman said: "My sister's gynecologist told her that she should date men who are either five years older or five years younger because men our own age are very confused. They grew up in a crazy period. The rules have been changed for these guys and they don't know how to react."

Dr. Noel Cazenave, a Temple University sociologist who researches sex roles, agrees. Men today, he says, "feel that their traditional identity badges and standards of performance are eroding, and as of yet, no new patterns have evolved to take their place. . . . Men are confused as to what kind of man women want them to be."

The confusion is most acute when it comes to sex. Some men are so unsure of how they should proceed that they do nothing. They're afraid to date, because they think women expect them to have sex the first night. In the past, when there was a reliable series of sexual steps—necking, petting, etc.—there was time for a relationship to develop. Today, everything is so wham-bang-thank-you-ma'am that it virtually precludes any progression from warmth to intimacy.

There's no question in my mind that having sex with someone, no matter how casual, changes the nature of a relationship. To take this step after only a few hours of acquaintanceship often means aborting a potential friendship. It can also mean short-circuiting the heart, for it's very difficult to be emotionally intimate with someone you don't yet know enough to trust. The few times I've climbed into bed with a virtual stranger, I've always climbed out the next morning with emotional indigestion. The ego thrill of the conquest never compensated for the empty, sticky feeling afterwards.

And yet, among sophisticated adults, first-date sex seems as *de rigueur* today as the kiss was a quarter century ago. When I first became single, I thought this new custom was wonderful. But it didn't take long before its appeal faded. Soon, occasions arose when I didn't want to share my body with a woman I hardly knew. I wanted to sleep in my own bed, by myself. Unfortunately, some of the women I dated were so used to instant sex that when I balked they were insulted. One night, for instance, a woman invited me to her place for dinner. The meal was good and we had an enjoyable time chatting afterwards. Although I found her attractive and interesting, I was not especially eager at that point to know her carnally. Shortly before midnight, I got up to leave. After muttering the usual parting banalities, I kissed her. "Is that all I get?" she said, looking genuinely hurt. I didn't know what to say. I was embarrassed and felt guilty. Incredibly, I had offended her by *not* making a pass at her.

Many of my male friends have related tales of similar awkward moments. And though we complain, sometimes less than ingenuously, about being put in such positions, we can't help but be amused by the turnabout. In the words of a single woman friend: "Because of the inevitability about having sex, men are the ones who are pulling back. Women are all for it and have come to view men as toys, sex objects, dildos. People have forgotten that man is supposed to be a hunter. When he's not doing the hunting, he rolls over and plays dead."

"Today, women have dropped much of their sexual reserve," writes Christopher Lasch in *The Culture of Narcissism.* "In the eyes of men, this makes them more accessible as sexual partners but also more threatening. Formerly men complained about women's lack of sexual response; now they find this response intimidating and agonize about their capacity to satisfy it."

"Many men regard today's woman as a multi-orgasmic supersex," says Dr. Mirta T. Mulhare, Dean of Arts, Sciences and Humanities at the State University of New York, College at Old Westbury and a professor in the Department of Biological Sciences and Community Health. "Men are so threatened by having to prove their masculinity that impotence among young males is very high. There is also a growing number of men suffering from retarded ejaculation, or 'Casanova's Disease.' These men are so eager to please women that they're afraid to let go and come."

It is unclear whether impotence is more common today than in the past or whether more men are simply admitting and reporting it. But I do know that many of my male friends have suffered anxiety about performing and that many of my woman friends are complaining about what seems like an impotence epidemic. It doesn't surprise me. After all, the penis is not just a piece of plumbing. In most men, it's controlled as much by the heart as the head, and if the feeling's not there, it's usually impossible to fake it. Many perfectly healthy, lusty men are stunned by this discovery, and the first experience can sometimes be so traumatic that just the memory of it handicaps them in the future.

There may be other factors at work, however. I suspect that many men today—sometimes consciously, more often unconsciously—are angry at women. Thanks to the women's movement, they feel dispossessed, stripped of their traditional rights and prerogatives. "Men are not up to dealing with the onslaught of competition from women," a single woman friend contends. "How can you sleep with a woman who reminds you of your mother, a creature who is capable, competent, invincible? Women today may be more wonderful, but today's man doesn't realize it. All he knows is that his bastion has been defiled, power has been taken away from him, and he hasn't been given anything in return." And what better way to get back at women than to not "be a man" in the most fundamental way? What could be more insulting to a woman's sense of womanliness than a man's remaining unaroused?

The irony of all this is that many women also feel victimized by the women's movement. "Women's lib has done a great disservice to women," a single woman I know said. "It's been great in terms of job equality, salaries and benefits, but when it comes to being treated nicely by men, I think it has torn down a lot of the old traditions that I'd like to see still standing."

"In a way, what happened in the sixties sort of backfired in our faces," a woman lawyer told me. "What women's liberation, and particularly the sexual revolution, did was make women more vulnerable to predatory men. I know many women who feel bitter about the women's movement. They feel they're not married now because of that."

Today, writes Lasch, "all women find themselves identified with 'women's lib' merely by virtue of their sex. . . . All women share in the burdens as well as the benefits of 'liberation,' both of which can be summarized by saying that men no longer treat women as ladies."

For the hard-charging professional woman, the situation is even worse. Many men shun such women either because they resent their success or because they assume that women of such high status would have no time for them. For example, a friend of mine who works for a television station finds men so intimidated by her that when she meets them in a bar she tells them she's a teacher.

Some women, though, are their own worst enemies. In my travels as a single man, I met several professional women who, in an attempt to prove themselves by outmacho-ing their male colleagues, behaved in a manner that was so smooth, efficient and impassive that it seemed deliberately designed to keep men at bay. I would argue, in fact, that if sexual impotence is epidemic among men today, emotional impotence is epidemic among women. In other words, there are a lot of women out there with hard heads and cold hearts—women who, as a male friend of mine put it, "don't want to be loved; they want to be promoted." Their resumes may be golden, and their careers jet-propelled, but their capacity to give and to love is about as small as their egos are large. "Some women have tried so hard to be taken seriously as a person that they've de-emphasized being a woman," says Dr. Brenda B. Bary, a Philadelphia clinical psychologist. "Now they find they're not being taken seriously as women." "It's no wonder that men are reticent," says Dr. Reed. "The young liberated woman often acts very cool and independent and doesn't seek to display any of the courtesies or rituals of interplay with men."

Often, the New Woman behaves this way simply because she's confused, as baffled about how to act and what to do as many men. "A lot of us are a lot more liberated in our heads than we are in our guts," says Dr. Bary. Anyone who has flipped through the pages of a women's magazine recently knows that macho is out and that the sensitive New Male is in. Yet many women concede there's a visceral part of them that misses the old macho man. One women's magazine calls it "the appeal of the heel." The basic axiom: "The man who means trouble is the man who means most." In a *Mademoiselle* article entitled "Why Nice Guys Finish Last with Women," Signe Hammer wrote: "After feminism, after self-help, assertiveness training and psychotherapy, women still want to be dominated. . . . The truth is, a lot of us are still looking for a hero. . . . We perceive power and energy as sexy, not gentleness and nurturing, which comes across somehow as passivity. . . . The powerful, dominating male seems to have what it takes, sexually. And, as females, it may be that we relate most deeply and atavistically not to the idea of actively seeking our own orgasm but to the delicious sense of being filled, the voluptuous passivity of satiation and completion."

In *Real Property,* author Sara Davidson makes the same point: "I often feel these days that I'm singing the reverse of what Rex Harrison sang in *My Fair Lady.* Why can't a man be more like a woman? I want men to be close to their feelings, intuitive, gentle, vulnerable and compassionate. I have known a few men who have been this way. There was only one problem. Sex with them was lousy."

After years of shaking my head in dismay over some of the men my mother chose as lovers, and after witnessing some of the wrongheaded escapades of some of my single women friends, it's hard not to believe that some women are simply masochists. I know two women, for example, who routinely get involved with married men or men who are very cruel to them. They know from the start that the relationship has no future, that there's absolutely no happy ending, and that instead of a ring they'll probably get the shaft, yet they plow right ahead. One of these women is exceptionally beautiful and she manages to attract her share of nice guys. But few of these men ever make it to first base, because as soon as they grow fond of her, she begins to detest them. The men who seem to catch her fancy the fastest and to hold it the longest are the rogues, bastards and outlaws. She finds them irresistibly magnetic and exciting, even as they are making her life deliciously miserable.

I've talked to women about this a lot, and many, after several glasses of wine, will admit that yes, there's some truth to it. Maybe it's the maternal instinct at work, a conviction that this charming rascal can be tamed and reformed. Or maybe it's just the fact that sex is somehow better when it's tinged with illicitness. But then, in the next breath, these same women will insist that no, that's not what they really want. What women *really* want, they'll say, is a long-lasting, loving relationship with a man. "We are romantic," writes *Boston*

FOUR

The False Promise of Sexual Freedom

A DIVORCED MAN:

When I got divorced, I was really looking forward to the freedom of being single. This would be my big chance to live out all my fantasies —a different lady every night of the week. I thought sex would be easy and free. My first disappointment came when I realized I was right. It was easy and free, too easy and free.

I got to try out all sorts of new positions. I saw a wonderful variety of female bodies. Hugh Hefner would have been proud of me. I can remember one time when I was seeing three different women at once. I was practically living out of my car, sleeping with one woman one night, another woman the next. Paradise, right? Guess again. One morning, I woke up and I didn't know where I was. I didn't know whose bed I was in or who I was with. What was I doing there? What was I trying to prove?

After that, I began to do some thinking. All this catting around was empty and meaningless. Sure, the sex was plentiful, but it was also so clinical, so aseptic, so perfunctory that for the first time in my life there were times when I had trouble getting it up. Sex was so available that it was too *easy. There was no resistance, no chase, no challenge, no sport, no romance. Some women were so aggressive that it was a hassle to keep them at bay. A few times I even wished I were married so they'd leave me alone, so I wouldn't have to worry about offending them by turning them down.*

What bothered me the most was that I just didn't feel good about myself. I felt like I was wasting my life. And gradually it became clear to me that you can't be a nice guy and a stud at the same time. Or at least I couldn't. To be a stud you have to be an emotional hit-and-run artist. You have to be willing to manipulate, mislead and deceive people. And if you're willing to do that kind of thing, then in my book at least, you're not a nice guy.

At the same time, I started realizing how much I missed the closeness of my marriage when things were good. When you're married, you can really become intimate. On an alphabetical scale, you might reach Point X or Y with your spouse. You know each other so well that you can communicate volumes with the subtlest look, gesture, even smell. When you're single and you're trying to play the field, you keep starting all over again with new people. Again, on an alphabetical scale, you never get past Point C or D. Everything is so tentative. Because you know so little about each other, there's little trust. And without trust, it's hard for there to be any real caring. I missed having someone really care about me. Pretty soon, I kind of dropped out of the singles scene. I was afraid of hurting others—and myself.

Shortly before I got married, I had a discussion about marriage with a woman friend who outspokenly opposes the institution.

"I'll never get married," she told me. "That's when the walls come closing in. That's when you kiss your freedom goodbye."

"Nobody's really free," I said. "You're always making choices that limit you in some way. When you take a job, you give up your freedom to drive a motorcycle across the country. When you decide to become a lawyer, you give up your freedom to be a doctor. When I'm married, I'll be able to do just about anything I can do now. The only thing I won't be able to do, if I take my marriage vow seriously, is have sex with another woman. In other words, I won't have the freedom to be promiscuous."

That was it, I thought later. The great freedom of singlehood was the freedom to act on your lust with any person at any time. It was the freedom to do just about anything two adults can do between sheets, except be intimate. For to stay free, you could not afford to become close. Because if you became close, you might begin to feel and care. And once feeling and caring get involved, things get serious. Before you know it, you might love. And love is the end of freedom. It's attachment, responsibility and commitment.

Psychoanalyst Erik Erikson contends that the critical task we face in our twenties is developing the capacity for intimacy—that is, learning "to commit [ourselves] to concrete affiliations and partnership and to develop the ethical strength to abide by such commitments." Sadly, commitment has been the Achilles' heel of the baby boom generation.

"It was able to commit itself politically and socially all right, to everything from Hula-Hoops to the protest movements," writes Landon Jones in *Great Expectations.* "Those commitments were made ensemble, *as a mass.* The baby boom's strongest and most effective statements have always come through the larger group. Only in the aggregate could they find the necessary intensity and emotion to fulfill their needs. But the baby boomers, so decisive and passionate as a generation, were practically paralyzed on the individual level. It was as if life in the here and now could not deliver on the expectations they had always had for it. Why should one limit one's prospects when the choices still ahead were so thrilling?"

But how thrilling is freedom, how free is freedom, when it becomes such a totem that it virtually disables you, preventing you from feeling and caring, loving and being loved? "Singlehood makes you free in the sense that your actions don't matter to anyone else," another single woman friend told me recently. "To not matter to anyone is not such a wonderful thing. Like the song says, 'Freedom's just another word for nothing left to lose.' "

"We cannot love without committing ourselves to another person," asserts Rollo May in *Freedom and Destiny*. "In grasping for freedom from entanglement with another person, we come to grief over our failure of compassion and commitment—indeed, the failure to love authentically. . . . To treat sex and values as totally divorced from each other is . . . to block the development of one's freedom. . . . Moral concern in sex hinges on the acceptance of one's responsibility for the other as well as for oneself. Other people do matter; and the celebration of this gives sexual intercourse its ecstasy, its meaning, and its capacity to shake us to our depths."

Without a doubt, being single can sometimes be glamorous, thrilling and full of adventure. But for most people, it's a temporary state, because ultimately, being single is unfulfilling. Most single people *do* want intimacy; they do want, as a single woman friend put it, "to have just one other person love them the best."

In *The Art of Loving,* a book about love and human relationships that has become a modern classic, Erich Fromm contends that the "deepest need of man is the need to overcome his separateness, to leave the prison of his aloneness." This "desire for interpersonal fusion . . . is the most fundamental passion, it is the force which keeps the human race together, the clan, the family, the society. The failure to achieve it means insanity or destruction—self-destruction or destruction of others."

The casualties are all around us: brittle, neurotic women whose longest, most successful relationships are with cats, and glib, feckless men whose chief aims in life are "scoring with chicks" and keeping their softball batting averages above .500.

"I don't think people were ever meant to live alone," a single woman said. "You get used to what you want becoming the only criteria for everything. It seems so sterile and calcifying. You become so stiff and unable to deal with real life.

"I have a friend who has a litmus test for the men she dates. If they move the bathroom rug from the tub to the sink and don't move it back, she gets furious. That's it; that's the end. She drops them. That's what can happen when you're single too long. You get out of the habit of the way the world is."

I wonder about some of my peers who've reached

their mid-thirties without finding anyone they can spend the rest of their lives with, or at least a few years with. Since college, their personal lives have consisted of a series of short-term affairs. By now, this lifestyle has become habitual. It may not be wrong in any moral or ultimate sense, but to me, jumping from one relationship to another is like being a newspaper reporter who jumps from story to story, always observing other people's problems from a detached perspective. After a while, your skin grows so tough that it dies.

"People who can best function in a system of sex without intimacy are those who have little capacity for feeling in the first place," argues Rollo May. "It is the persons who are compulsive and mechanical in their reactions—in short, the ones who operate like nonsentient motors."

To escape their "prison of aloneness," many people today seek connection through casual sex. But this search, warns Erich Fromm, eventually "results in an ever-increasing sense of separateness, since the sexual act without love never bridges the gap between two human beings, except momentarily."

And so they go on searching, festooning their egos with new accessories, repackaging their personalities, mastering new erotic tricks, adding new war stories to their psychic histories—wounded and frightened, careening through life with their sexual accelerators pressed to the floor and their emotional clutch pedals in, they eschew intimacy, keeping their encounters free of affect, going back to the savage for their sensations, cauterizing their hearts and debasing their souls in their wild rut-boar wallowing, losing freedom the more they seek it, scouring every bar, every party, every business meeting for Mr. Right, or the woman with the right chemistry, all the while denying that the problem of love is not only the problem of an *object* but also the problem of a *faculty.*

A remarried man:

After I got divorced, I was absolutely anti-marriage. Marriage was insanity to me, since it had brought me nothing but grief. My inclination at that point was being bolstered by a lot of anti-marriage literature. Feminists were attacking the very premise of marriage. If I had free-associated with the word "marriage" then, I would have come up with words like "prison," "suffocation," "boredom."

After a while, I got involved with a woman I really enjoyed. We began living together even though I wasn't interested in monogamy. Honesty is very important to me, so I wasn't interested in cheating. I didn't want to undermine the relationship that way. Instead, I started dating other women openly and undermined the relationship head-on.

I began dating again and fell into the search-for-the-perfect-woman syndrome. After a while, it was almost like conducting job interviews. There were a lot of one-date situations. I'd go out with promising people and realize that they weren't what they pretended to be. There was a lot of false advertising. . . .

I met one woman who was beautiful, intelligent, rich and very loose. She had the money to fly off to the Virgin Islands or Aspen. She seemed to have men scattered all over the country, and I guess I was her man in Philadelphia. She was very reluctant to say where she'd been and very uncomfortable with total honesty.

She was so scared to death of real intimacy that she made me look like Joe Steady. In fact, she was a caricature of me. She brought all my quirks into high relief and made me realize how absurd they were. Because she was so uncomfortable with herself most of the time, she made me realize that comfort was a real high priority for me. She made me realize that I didn't always want to be moving on. I wanted an oasis, a place to relax and be at peace. She was always plunging into a storm, often a very interesting storm, but who needs it?

Now I've come to a point where I've realized that all the negatives I saw before were actually positives. I've come to understand that marriage means more freedom not less. It means a different kind of adventure, wherein the lack of variety is made up for by the intensity of the experience with a single human being. As for sex, it's just a lot more fun when you are sharing it with someone you really care about.

The great irony of the last two decades is that the search for fulfillment through sexual freedom, which wrecked so many marriages, did not, in the end, degrade marriage, which had been so maligned, but sex (or more properly, erotic love) which had been so exalted. Today sex has become a mere sport, a recreation that, in the words of a woman I know, "combines the best of squash and gourmet cooking, with no calories." It's been "divorced not only from love and creation but also from empathy, compassion, morality, responsibility, and sometimes even common politeness," asserts George Leonard in his provocative book *The End of Sex.* "It has become something you 'have.' You have a car, you have dinner, you have a swim, you have the chicken pox . . . and you have sex."

That sex has become so trivialized is a tragedy, because sex, I believe, is sacred—not in a religious or sacramental sense, but in the sense John Updike was getting at when, in *Couples,* he described lovemaking as "an exploration of a sadness so deep people must go in pairs, one cannot go alone." Because we are more than dumb animals, because we also have minds and feelings and souls, sex is so much more than merely a reflex. It is an ineffable force, infinite in its mysteries and profound in its effects. Think of it: When we are our most animal, we can also be our most emotional and spiritual.

"For whatever else is in the act, lust, cruelty, the desire to dominate, or whole delights of desire, the result can be no more than a transaction—pleasurable, even all-encompassing, but a transaction—when no hint remains of the awe that a life in these circumstances can be conceived," argues Norman Mailer in *The Prisoner of Sex.*

To me, casual recreational sex is nothing more than mutual masturbation. Although two bodies may be involved, the intercourse is usually only physical and devoid of the deep emotional exchanges that accompany intimacy. Hence, the experience is fundamentally a lonely, solipsistic one. As George Leonard notes, casual sex is "hardly a feast—not even a good, hearty sandwich. It is a diet of fast food served in plastic containers. Life's feast is available only to those who are willing and able to engage life on a deeply personal level, giving all, holding back nothing."

It's ironic to me that in popular culture the womanizer is sometimes depicted as a sexual adventurer, someone with moxie, daring and the swashbuckling courage of a frontier explorer. In truth, many studs and libertines are nothing more than cowards—pathetic, rootless people who are desperately afraid to open themselves, to become intimate, to take the risks of a commitment. Far from demonstrating prowess, their promiscuity is an attempt to escape from emotional complexity, an attempt to achieve a strict separation between sex and feeling. In some circles, this kind of escape is lauded as liberation, yet another milestone in our progress from the dark days of sexual repression. Today's hip ideology of "nonbinding commitments" and "cool sex" has made "a virtue of emotional disengagement," says Christopher Lasch. As a result, sexual liaisons, including marriage, are terminated easily, and true intimacy has become more elusive than ever.

A separated man:

After my wife and I broke up, I tried to be a single man, even though I wasn't really interested in casual sex. . . . There was a woman at work who started coming on to me. She was a friend and I admired her work and I appreciated her being attracted to me, but I wasn't particularly attracted to her. At one point, she came right out and suggested we have sex. She said we didn't have to get seriously involved because she was committed to somebody else.

I was reticent, but she kept pushing. 'Why don't you try it and see if you like it?' she said. I gave in and had satisfying physical experiences on numerous occasions, but I never felt that great about it. Instead of reassuring me that I should be content with the physical pleasure and delighted to have that kind of relationship, she became emotionally involved with me and started casting me in the role of a heavy. At that point, I turned on my heels and fled. . . .

Casual sex has never been that satisfying or enjoyable to me. Really passionate sex occurs spontaneously in the context of affection for someone. . . . In dispassionate sex, I've always felt more like a performer than a person. It wasn't really me, this creature who needs to be held, cuddled and stroked, but some detached third party, a possessor of erotic tools and bits of knowledge about how to please a woman's body. . . .

If anything, my experiences with casual sex have intensified my positive feelings about marriage. I realize this is a radical statement, but sex is first and foremost a way to perpetuate the human race. If you get too far away from that natural imperative, then I think you're not using your body—or your soul, for that matter—the way it was meant to be used.

For me, the end came one night when I was having dinner with a date and suddenly, like a character in a Woody Allen movie, heard myself talking. What a bore! I was tired of hearing my voice tell the same old stories about my past, about growing up, my family, my first marriage, my impressions of the singles scene, my interests and hobbies, hopes and dreams, fears and insecurities. By then, I was also tired of hearing everybody else's same old stories. And I was tired of waking up in strange beds with strange women, women I had slept with in many cases more because I thought it was expected than because of any great desire. It was no longer any fun. It was work, *hard* work. And for what? So I could wake up at forty and find myself still single —a dotty, cranky, selfish old bachelor with nothing to show for my personal life but a thick black book full of the names of budding bimbos and aging neurotics? I began wishing I were at home, by myself, with a good book and a good woman who loved me as much as I loved her. I began wishing for a wife.

FIVE

In Search of the Perfect Mate

A SHORT WHILE AGO, A bachelor friend of mine came east from California to visit his family and friends. He is now in his early thirties, and if you met him at a party, you'd probably envy him. He is, to begin with, extraordinarily good-looking. He has matinee-idol features—prominent cheekbones, a square chin, white and even teeth, platinum blond hair—and he keeps his body tan, trim and muscular by jogging and playing lots of tennis. He is also intelligent, articulate, socially graceful and, with people he trusts, quite thoughtful and sensitive. Finally, thanks to some shrewd real estate investments, he is also a millionaire. But my friend is not content. During a conversation, he told me that he feels empty and that he was seriously considering moving back east, to some place inhabited by "real people with real values." He was tired of California and its perpetual sunshine and illusions, he said. He was tired too, he insisted, of women who are gorgeous on the outside but hollow on the inside.

At the moment, my friend has no intention of getting married, and he's not looking for a wife, but he worries at times about his inability to find a woman he can truly love, someone who is so wonderful that he'd gladly give up the pleasures and conveniences of bachelorhood for the privilege of her constant company.

"It's very difficult, if not impossible, to find someone who combines most, if not all, of the things you're looking for," he told me. "Like a lot of people, I'm basically looking for that perfect mate. Ironically, the problem's compounded because women are so accessible. It's crazy. Women pick up the guys these days. I've had women send drinks to my table or walk up to me and hand me their business cards. There's so much to choose from that I sometimes feel like a spinning top. I find myself having such a good time with different women for different reasons that it makes it very difficult to think of settling down with only one."

My friend is not alone. Many single men today are suffering from an embarrassment of riches. There are so many women to choose from that, like a kid in a candy store, they don't know where to start. Frozen by indecision, spurred on by lust, they often bounce from one casual encounter to the next. Eventually, this behavior can become so ingrained that by the time they're ready to settle down, they've become incorrigible lechers, unable not only to sustain an intimate relationship but also to find anyone they consider a worthy partner. Sure, there are lots of terrific women out there, but no sooner do they get to know one than they discover a flaw. She squeezes the toothpaste tube from the top, she's afraid of the dark, her voice is squeaky, her father is a drunk, she's got lines around her mouth, stretch marks on her breasts and the backs of her legs look like cottage cheese. Having waited this long, there's no way these men will go off into the sunset with anyone who's less than a goddess.

Another friend of mine, a man who was quite a swinger before he remarried, calls it the "perfect-mate syndrome," and from what I can see, it's become epidemic among the unmarried today. Having spent their twenties and, in some cases, their thirties dating around, they've become so discriminating that no human being could possibly meet their standards. Some yearn for mates who resemble the unreal, plastic icons of movie and television screens. Others dream of a spouse who is nothing less than a composite of the best qualities of all their erstwhile lovers. If only she had Sally's laugh, and Sarah's legs, and Leslie's mind, and Ann's abandon, and Lisa's tennis game, and Cathy's sense of humor, and Janet's face, and Jill's breasts, and Becky's hair, and Vicky's education. The sad truth, however, is that for many this pursuit of the perfect mate is nothing more than an elaborate exercise in self-deception.

"For many bright and beautiful twenty-eight- to thirty-five-year-olds, this idea of the perfect mate has become paralyzing," says Sally Green, director of education at the Marriage Council of Philadelphia and a lecturer in psychiatry at the University of Pennsylvania School of Medicine. "They imagine this composite person with ideal qualities without looking at themselves and asking themselves whether such a person is truly a suitable match. Many do it as a defense against their fear of choosing and making a commitment. It's a way of dealing with their fear of failure. So Sue tells herself, If only John had a better income, I'd marry him. But then when John's income improves, Sue suddenly notices that his teeth aren't straight."

"The biggest reason people shy away from marriage—including myself—is commitment," my California friend confessed. "I personally don't relish the idea of making that kind of commitment, especially if I do so in a religious setting, and then breaking it. I know there are many people who get married thinking from Day One that they're going to have all the action on the side they can get. But I can't operate that way. Because of the way I grew up, if I make a commitment, I'd have a tough time living with myself if I broke it.

So there's a lot of pressure involved in marriage, and sometimes the easiest way to deal with it is the chicken's way—to dodge it. I have feathers all over me, let me tell you."

The perfect-mate syndrome is appealing not only because it's such a handy way to avoid commitment, but also because the fantasizing so intrinsic to it can be so pleasant. Here, for example, is how Lee Eisenberg envisioned the perfect mate in a 1980 *Esquire* article, "Looking for a Wife":

> There is a persistent image: a beach in summertime, late afternoon. There is a majestic Victorian house on a bluff, and it is filling up madly with children, the kids of the house and friends of those kids. On the patio, the adults have gathered, and they are pouring gin. The talk is animated, not of debentures or charity drives but of decent new novels and the tightening pennant race. . . .
>
> At center stage, framed against the stately house and the sunset beyond, is a woman with her hair tied back. She ranges inside and out, attending to the adults, keeping watch on the kids.
>
> She is a woman who can do an uncanny impersonation of Katharine Hepburn, but never in public. She is a woman who calls her sometimes overbearing husband "a jerk, but

> my kind of jerk." She is a woman who knows the names not only of trees and birds but of three-fourths of the players in the major leagues. She is a woman who can take yesterday's leftover tuna fish and keep nine kids quiet for twenty minutes. She is a woman who can take one glance at the steaks on the grill and tell her husband that if he leaves them on for one more second they'll taste like penny loafers. She is a woman who, every year, rereads Thomas Hardy. She is a woman who likes tennis but loathes tennis dresses. She is a woman who has made reckless love to enough men to know she isn't curious anymore. And she is a woman whose greatest regret—now that she is old enough to understand—is that she never made peace with her father while he was alive.

Finding such a wonderful woman is not easy, however. Her lucky husband, Eisenberg reveals, "waited and waited long."

> Through hundreds of dinners with dozens of women, he waited. Through summer weekends in the mountains, vacations in Greece, sleepless nights in funky motels, he waited. Killing time, he mixed them drinks, took them sailing, cried in their arms. He

asked them to brunch, kissed them on New Year's Eve, sent them roses on their birthdays. He told a select few that he loved them and he met their parents. But things came unglued, or he unglued them, or let Sally or Chris or Jenny or Margaret unglue them.

In the meantime, he learned. Oh boy, did he! He learned to measure them up in the blink of an eye, to waste neither time nor money on the obvious losers. What a quick study he became! The curve of her neck, the taste of her lips, the nature of her sadness: he knew in a blink whether he should move in closer on Anna or Jane. What an eye for fine points! He rated their taste in shoes. He rated their grasp of current events. He rated their physical fitness. He rated their opinions of movies and books. He rated their genes and the genes of their forebears. It got so he could rate them as surely and swiftly as an experienced trainer rates thoroughbreds (not that they all were, to be sure). His goal was to pick a winner, a sure thing, someone to go wire-to-wire. His goal was to find the legs, heart, and bloodline of a champion, all in tip-top condition, all amounting to . . . *wife material.*

The syndrome, of course, is not limited to men. Many single women I know have rejected marriage offers from perfectly decent guys because they're holding out for the mythical Mr. Right, who is nothing less than a fabulous pastiche of romantic heroes from movies, novels and television shows. "I so rarely meet a man whom I have a crush on," an attractive television reporter told me. "I'd love to be swept off my feet by a guy who makes me think, God, I'm going to have four orgasms just looking at him."

Indeed, a charge often leveled against the most eligible single women is that they are whining perfectionists whose standards for men are too high and uncompromising. "Women today sometimes tend to be too demanding of men," says Dr. Brenda Bary, the Philadelphia clinical psychologist. "They assume that because they're this perfect phenomenon, then naturally they have to have a perfect man, an unflawed specimen." Or, as one women's magazine put it, "When princesses have rising expectations, it's harder than ever to be the prince."

"I think it's unfair when articles come down so hard on men, because often we're to blame," a woman lawyer admitted to me. "I've rejected men who are nice because they're not physically attractive or because their jobs are not up to what I consider worthy of myself. I can't say that there aren't any good men around, but I can say that there aren't many men whom I consider equal to me in occupation and looks."

Like their male counterparts, these women are sometimes so picky that it's questionable whether they sincerely wish to have a relationship. "A woman may look like she is ready for a relationship," says Dr. Bary, "but very often the truth is that she's afraid of intimacy and what it will cost to share her life, the compromises and sacrifices that are required."

How did things come to such a sorry pass? Obviously, many factors are involved, but in my opinion, too little attention has been paid to the role of the media —television, movies, radio, records, advertising, magazines, newspapers and books. Collectively, the media have unprecedented power to disseminate new ideas, images and products. Increasingly, the media are supplanting the family, school and the church in establishing norms and sanctioning mores. Significantly, since the media are constantly vying for our attention, they are compelled to seek out, exploit and hype the latest, the glitziest, the most sensational. And in many, sometimes not-so-subtle, ways, the media are affecting our sense of reality.

I'm convinced, for example, that the blatant salaciousness of pop music has reduced sex to a body function about as exalted as burping or sweating. I believe that the evanescence of television has made all of us less patient, that the hugeness of the movie screen has made all of us long for romantic partners who are larger than life. I believe too that the advertising industry has trained us to value surface attributes and has fostered the notion that everything can and should be replaced by a new and better model.

"I hold the media partly responsible for my predicament today," an unmarried woman friend of mine said. "When we were growing up, television filled our heads with all these images of romantic heroes, men who were handsome, dynamic, sensitive and intelligent. We grew up with all these expectations that could never be fulfilled. Real life and real men aren't that way, and it's created a lot of disappointment and disillusionment." How many men, after all, have the rugged good looks of Robert Redford, the sophisticated polish of Cary Grant, the steadfast character of Gregory Peck, the personal style of Humphrey Bogart? Who can compete with Richard Gere, Burt Reynolds or Tom Selleck, especially since on the TV or movie screen they're *performing,* and hence their natural magnetism is magnified, their personalities presented in the most flattering, heroic light?

Among men, the inclination to play the field and date several women at once is encouraged by magazines such as *Playboy,* which seduces its readers each month with a new, impossibly gorgeous Playmate—

her moles, wrinkles and other imperfections airbrushed away—while extolling the sybaritic lifestyle of the eternal bachelor. Meanwhile, the plots of more and more movies and popular television shows, such as *Falcon Crest*, *Dallas* and *Dynasty*, revolve around adultery, which is presented as an exciting, fashionable, sophisticated pastime. There is little hint that by undermining marriage adultery undermines the family, the basic unit of society. But why let stodgy moral considerations get in the way of entertainment and ratings and money?

"Many of the students in my classes today tell me that the Seventh Commandment is obsolete," says Sally Green. "Their concept of monogamy allows for what they call 'flings,' short sexual liaisons that 'don't count' because they supposedly don't intrude on the primary relationship. If I were a young person today, I'd be scared to get married, because marriage as an institution, as something with transcendent value and meaning to our society and culture, does not get much positive reinforcement from the media."

Consider the kind of people who work for the media. From my own experience, I can say that many are "progressive" or "liberal" in outlook. Some have a passionate personal interest in promoting new ideas and trends. Some are former counterculture types who are contemptuous of traditional institutions simply because they're not revolutionary. Some are members of what Brigitte and Peter Berger, authors of *The War Over the Family,* call the "knowledge class"—arrogant experts and technocrats, often long on cosmic ideals and short on personal scruples, who believe their intellectual sophistication exempts them from conventional morality. Some are transplanted small-towners who, embarrassed by their own middle-classness, are trying to live down any suspicion of Babbittry by affecting a swank, with-it urban worldliness. And some, finally, are simply sensation-mongers, adventure addicts who bounce from event to event, story to story, and often, in their romantic lives, person to person. When political scientists S. Robert Lichter and Stanley Rothman surveyed 240 journalists at what are widely regarded as the nation's most influential media institutions—the *New York Times,* the *Washington Post,* the *Wall Street Journal, Time, Newsweek, U.S. News and World Report,* the three commercial television networks, and public television—I was not surprised that they found that 54 percent do not regard adultery as wrong, and only 15 percent strongly agree that extramarital affairs are immoral.

The ramifications of this are disturbing. While those in the media may not be trying to undermine marriage deliberately, they may be undermining it unwittingly simply by ignoring its positive aspects and its importance as a social institution. Today, says Sally Green, "There's very little attention given to marriage as an important means of preserving and passing on our cultural and religious heritage. There's very little hype for marriage as a social or religious contract—a sanctification, a holiness. And if you don't glorify it, if marriage as an institution has no greater meaning, how can you justify a relationship where there's so much giving in and sacrificing? If you're going to ask me to clean up crap from my husband and kids for fifty years, I want to know what's the greater good. Where's the glory? I don't see it out there today. Nobody's clapping their hands."

Paradoxically, even though marriage is by far the norm in our society, the media have so glamorized the risqué and avant-garde that many married adults, including myself, feel like wallflowers and losers who are missing out on all the fun. In a nationwide poll of more than a thousand men and women between 18 and 60, most of whom were married, psychiatrist George Serban of New York University found that their greatest source of stress was the changes in society's attitudes toward sex, including sexual permissiveness.

"I sometimes resent the fact that the single people I know seem to be sleeping with everybody and his brother and that they're on display so much," a male friend of mine said. "That kind of lifestyle is so celebrated today that it puts tremendous pressure on a marriage. When you're having problems at home and the single guy at the desk next to you is fielding phone calls from all his horny girlfriends, it sometimes makes you wonder what kind of fool you are.

"The Hite figure on adultery among married men says it all. It shows how susceptible married men are to the lures of being single. And what it says about our society is that we haven't come very far from the Romans."

At the same time that the media are undermining marriage by making it seem unhip and unexciting, they are also promoting a sense of values—false values, I contend—that are ultimately inimical to marriage. Because television, for example, is a visual medium, it specializes in presenting the visually pleasing. Therefore, it is a medium that worships beauty, youth and flash. It idealizes the ever-smiling, blow-dried actors who read the local news. It deifies curvy starlets like Farrah Fawcett, Loni Anderson and Joan Collins. (When was the last time you saw a TV camera pan the crowd at a football game and linger over the face of a hook-nosed, saggy-cheeked, baggy-eyed fifty-year-old?).

Managed by slick network executives, who often

have the attention span of a housefly and all the thoughtfulness of a tadpole, television is a medium that honors style over substance, appearance over reality. It is a medium that has truly amplified show business, with the emphasis on *show.* It is a medium of the here and now, where time is critical, where nothing can be permitted to drag or become boring, lest someone in Dubuque switch the channel. It is a medium of instant feedback, an other-directed, always-seeking-to-please, morally relativistic, nice-guy medium, ever attuned to ratings, always running in a popularity contest that will determine what it will look like and do next.

Inevitably, some of these values have rubbed off on those who watch TV. And so, when many men and women today are looking for a mate, the narcissistic principle that guides them is: Who I am with is a reflection of who I am. And so they worry: Is Nancy as beautiful as I am? Does she dress with the right style? Do we make a dynamite couple when we walk into a room? And: Is Rick's resume as impressive as mine? Does he make enough money? Is he a success? How well does he work an office party? Does he have any weird habits that might embarrass me, that will ruin our show?

In such a climate, it's no wonder cosmetic surgery is booming, for the worst thing that can happen to a woman, and especially a wife, is to grow old, ugly and fat. "I'm always seeing men in their fifties who've fallen in love with twenty-five-year-olds," says Sally Green. "They'll come in here and tell me their thirty-year marriage was nothing. When I meet their new loves, the interesting thing is that they're always knockouts. In fact, I've rarely seen an ugly one, a plain one, or even a simple one."

Unfortunately, relationships and marriages founded on surface attributes rarely endure. In truth, the superficial qualities that seem to fuel our infatuations often have little to do with why we seek to mate. Sally Green says, "People probably still wind up getting attached and coupling for deep psychodynamic reasons that they're totally unaware of. To assume that we have free will in this matter is really a *folie.* A good part of it is unconscious, somewhat irrational, and probably has more to do with psychological needs, pheromones, hormones and timing than having matching resumes or the same taste in clothes or movies."

In the end, then, the search for the perfect mate is doomed to futility not only because perfect people don't exist, despite the efforts of the media to convince us otherwise, but also because we really have very little control over the search to begin with. It takes a while for most people to realize this. After all, it's hard to admit that our free will isn't that free, and that real-life heroes are few and far between and often not very pleasant to live with. For journalist and best-selling author Nora Ephron, coming to this realization took two marriages and two divorces. Asked by a newspaper reporter what she now wants in a man, she replied: "What I like, and what I want, is the day-to-dayness of a relationship that's very solid and trusting. I would love, just *love* the sort of pokey, bourgeois, eat-in-the-kitchen, pork chops-again, do-you-want-a-salad?, no-don't-bother kind of life, and my idea of a really great evening is to crawl into bed and watch television. Romantic fantasies have to alter, you know. The dashing whoever who was going to sweep you off in his private jet—you can't do it anymore. All the stuff you used to imagine would be the most wonderful way to live—well, it isn't anymore."

For me, the epiphany came one raw, windy November day a few years ago when I was installing new wooden storm windows on my old stone farmhouse in rural Bucks County, Pennsylvania. It was one of those bittersweet fall days when just to be outside was to be reminded of the inexorable passage of the seasons, of time, of life itself. The ground was brown and hard, the trees silver and bare, and periodically, flocks of geese in perfect V formation would honk by in the pewter sky. By mid-afternoon, my fingers were numb as I con-

SIX

The Joy of Being a Giver

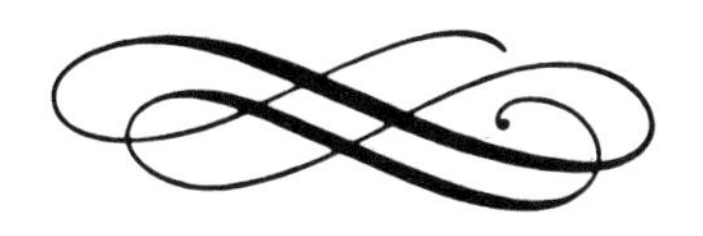

SO MANY NEWSPAPERS, MAGazines and books are full of information about the *problems* of marriage that one sometimes wonders why anyone in his or her right mind would be crazy enough ever to consider it. Who needs all the hassles? What's the percentage in entering a social contract that involves so much time and hard work?

A few years ago, when it became obvious that my relationship with my girlfriend Tanya was headed toward marriage, I wrestled with these questions myself. My attitude towards marriage then was typical of the newly divorced—to wit, once burned, twice shy. Did I really want to do it again? I asked myself. Did I really want to give up my freedom? Did I really want to make such an important commitment? Was it worth it?

In the course of trying to answer these questions, I woke up one night with an "anxiety attack." Whether the attack had been precipitated by my ambivalence about marriage, or some other worry, I don't know, but in an effort to fall asleep again, I began enumerating the good things about marriage, drawing in many cases from happy memories of my first marriage and observations of the solid marriages of friends and acquaintances. After only an hour, I had listed enough good points about marriage to fill several pages in a legal-size tablet.

First and foremost, I thought, the joy of marriage is the joy of not being alone. It is the joy of

—companionship and intimacy and having a person and place to come to;
—structure and order, comfort, security and stability;
—having someone to help with the burdens and drudgery of daily life;
—making a home and creating a family;
—being a parent and raising children.

It is the joy of

—defining your relationship with respect to others and society at large;
—loving someone so much that you want to celebrate that love and commitment publicly;

—taking a risk, making a leap of faith, going all the way;
—believing in someone and something above and beyond yourself;
—building something lasting and substantial.

It is the joy of

—having a best friend who is also your lover, and a lover who is also your best friend;
—sleeping with someone who warms your heart as well as your bed;
—making love without awkwardness, self-consciousness or shame;
—developing a private vocabulary and doing some of your best talking without words.

It is the joy of

—having someone real to hold when you wake up sweating during a dark night of the soul;
—having someone who truly cares, someone who will stand by you when you get sick, or falter or fail;
—having someone you believe in, and who believes in you, tell you at times that you're the best, and at other times, that you can be much better.

It is the joy of

—outgrowing your adolescent self-absorption and getting on with life;
—being faithful and honoring a vow;
—ennobling yourself through discipline and sacrifice;
—having a common history and mutual memories and the sense of having traveled together far;
—being a separate individual and yet also part of a whole;
—fighting and making up, going apart and coming together again;
—learning to yield and to compromise, to care and to love.

Finally, the joy of marriage is the joy of giving. To the jaded, it may sound trite and hackneyed, like some middle-brow bromide from the advice columns on the women's pages, but it's true: It's more blessed, or at least more satisfying, to give than to receive. For in giving we tap those parts of our being that make us special, noble, transcendent. In giving we exercise the most glorious powers of human nature. In giving we dispense grace. We dignify ourselves, we become almost divine. And in my opinion, there are few endeavors that demand more giving than a vital, working marriage.

"As your marriage progresses, what happens is you begin to feel you're creating something that's somehow bigger than either you or your husband," said a woman friend. "When you begin giving up something to the idea of the two of you, then a magical process occurs when you begin getting back more than you're giving. Then you gain a little confidence and give again, and back it comes again, and it begins to grow. The two of you are still there as individuals but there's also this blossoming entity that is the two of you as a couple. . . .

"Day by day, if you want the marriage to go on, you give in, you keep making decisions over and over again that this marriage is more important than this or that wish or desire. When you get into the habit of that, it makes you a good team, and in the end, it can make you a more gracious person. You get bigger; something about your whole life gets bigger."

Most of us are takers when we're young. We take from our parents and our teachers, from our churches and all the other institutions that nurture us to adulthood. My parents, for all their problems as a couple, were very generous people, and they gave abundantly to me. I'll never forget the many hours my father spent helping me build model train layouts or prepare projects for school science fairs. I'll always remember the presents he used to give me when he came home from business trips, and the high-jump standards he bought me when I became interested in track and field. I'll never forget the many hours my mother used to slave over her typewriter at night, preparing manuscripts for students and professors so she'd have the money to send me to private school. Or the time she gave me the family car, which she could have sold for badly needed cash, so I'd have something to drive at college. Later, when I graduated, she gave me an airplane ticket to Europe, which she'd bought by secret scrimping and saving.

I'll always remember the many kindnesses of my grandfather, and especially the summer he took me to Maine and showed me how to use woodworking tools and build boats and fire a gun and operate an outboard. And how could I forget the many teachers who took a special interest in me—the one who gave me books from his personal library, the one who took me to a museum on Saturday, the one who introduced me to classical music, the one who gave me a three-year "scholarship" to his summer camp, the one who invited me over for dinner and a talk when I was having troubles at home. Then there were the institutions, the Episcopal Academy and

Princeton, which gave me large amounts of financial aid so I could pursue my education in an atmosphere of excellence.

I have much to be grateful for. And now, having grown up, I recognize my obligation to begin giving back. But it's an obligation not unique to me. For central to achieving maturity is passing from being a taker to being a giver. As adults, we have the power, finally, to give back, to pay off our social debts, and so we give to our spouses, and our children, and our parents, and we begin to care for the institutions that cared for us so that future generations can enjoy the same benefits we did.

One of the advantages of marriage is that it encourages you, or forces you, to become a giver, because your marriage won't last long if you're a taker. Although my married friends have many faults, most of them seem to have one admirable trait in common. They are givers; they are on the credit side of society's ledger. In reaching this state, they have had to acknowledge the facts of life: that they are limited and fallible, that aging and death are inevitable, that they are human beings and that part of our human destiny is to be part of a community. In learning to give and to love, they have, as a woman friend put it, "yielded to the river of life."

Giving inevitably involves some degree of self-denial, but, as Daniel Yankelovich writes in *New Rules*, "Suppression of needs is not always bad. In fact, some suppression is required if one is to avoid becoming a blob of contradictions. The Christian injunction that to find one's self one must first lose oneself contains an essential truth any seeker of self-fulfillment must grasp."

"Really, what do people want?" asked an unmarried woman friend during a recent conversation about marriage. "They want to be loved and to love other people. By love, I mean thinking, willing and doing good of another. If you can be good to someone, you can really build something. That's where transcendence is, where you're carried out of the self, where you're really up there."

"Giving is the highest expression of potency," writes Erich Fromm in *The Art of Loving*. "In the very act of giving, I experience my strength, my wealth, my power. This experience of heightened vitality and potency fills me with joy. I experience myself as overflowing, spending, alive, hence as joyous. Giving is more joyous than receiving, not because it is a deprivation, but because in the act of giving lies the expression of my aliveness."

Indeed, who wants to spend life as a taker, passive and dependent like a child, when by growing into givers, we can become active and independent—like gods.

SEVEN

The Adventure of Intimacy

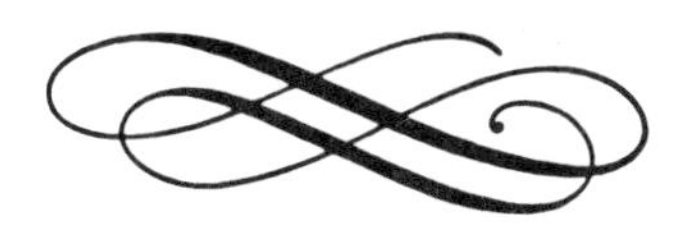

ON THE OPENING PAGE of D. H. Lawrence's *Women in Love,* Ursula Brangwen, one of the main characters, confesses to her sister Gudrun that she is wary of marriage because she fears that, instead of being an experience, marriage will more likely mean "the end of experience."

Many of my single friends share this view. They regard marriage as something you do when you run out of libidinal steam, when you tire of sampling the smorgasbord of life and love, when you grow so old and lazy that the soothing comforts of hearth and home become more attractive than the bright lights and action of the fast lane. In other words, marriage is something you do when you're ready for the end of adventure.

I disagree. In the words of a friend, a man who is now working to save his marriage: "Instead of closing off adventure, you're actually opening yourself to one of the greatest challenges you'll ever meet, the challenge of making a relationship work and endure. To deny yourself that challenge and the satisfaction you get when you succeed at it, in order to keep your options open in the hope that the Cheryl Tiegs of your dreams will someday throw herself at your feet, is to miss out on one of the best things life has to offer."

"When people say that so-and-so just got married for security, that's not right," said another friend, a married woman. "Marriage is often a way of putting yourself at a risk that is much greater than the risk you experience when you're single. The person you're married to can hurt you much more emotionally than anybody else. Opening yourself to that kind of vulnerability is part of what you give when you get married, and it's partly from that risk that growth comes."

"The ultimate erotic challenge," contends George Leonard in *The End of Sex*, "lies not in racing from bed to bed, shirttails aflame, but in the quest of what I call High Monogamy: a long-term relationship in which both partners are *voluntarily* committed to erotic exclusivity, not because of moral or religious scruples, not because of timidity or inertia, but because it is what they *want.* Because they seek excitement and adventure through the love of another person."

But can you find excitement and adventure through the love of the same person after five, ten, or twenty-five years of marriage? Can you stay interested in that person after passion and romance fade, as they inevitably do?

The answer is yes, some people can—people who believe that human beings are wondrously infinite in their complexity and mystery, and that despite our surface consistency, we are always changing, continually remaking our characters and souls. If you subscribe to these beliefs, then it is possible to have an endlessly exciting adventure with the same person, the adventure of intimacy.

What is this adventure, exactly? It is the kind of adventure you have when you spend a month-long vacation in Europe exploring one country in depth instead of visiting ten countries for only three days each. By confining yourself to one country, you do not deprive yourself of new discoveries, surprises and delights. If anything, these experiences are heightened because, through time and familiarity, you've gained a context. You've developed bearings, a sense of history and evolution and identity. Suddenly your adventures have meaning.

"When you travel," a male friend told me, "you see a lot, but only on a superficial level. Part of me wants to sink roots into everything I get hold of. I want to really know it, to go deeper instead of wider. I remember reading once about a Japanese writer who spent his entire life taking pictures in his own backyard. Some people can focus on the narrowest slice of life and find a whole universe. The problem with spreading yourself out is that you also spread yourself thin."

In pursuing the adventure of intimacy, at least half the thrill comes from finding out about yourself. Leonard says that the High Monogamist must have "a sort of towering, vertiginous daring. For this state requires that we look directly and unflinchingly at our every weakness and flaw, straight down through layer after layer of cowardice and self-deception to the very heart of our intentionality. . . . High Monogamy, merciless in its presentation of self-knowledge, demands that we change, that we have the courage to lead an essentially unpredictable life."

Before Tanya and I became close, I thought I was a pretty wonderful guy. Any woman lucky enough to snare me would be damn lucky, I believed. Then, as Tanya and I became intimate, as we began spending more time together, I realized what a Grade A jerk I could be—thoughtless, inconsiderate, selfish, moody. Alone, these faults never occurred to me, because there was no one to bump against, no check on my behavior, no limit on my whims and desires. But Tanya's responses to my excesses and lapses held up a mirror that often contained a very surprising, unflattering image. Just by being near me and loving me, she challenged me to change and to grow. Now that we're married, the process continues, and both of us are the better for it. As a married man put it in a recent issue of *Esquire:* "Marriage is like boxing; you can run but you can't hide. Sooner or later, you're going to end up in a clinch —and it's in the clinches where you learn the most about yourself, where your strength is really tested."

In another issue of *Esquire,* a man is quoted by "Ethics" columnist Laurence Shames: "I read somewhere that wolves mate for life. Which sort of surprised me, because I used to have this nagging feeling that it was the adventurous wolflike side of me that wanted to keep my options open, and the more passive, meeker side of me that craved the closeness and security of being with just one woman. Now I think it's just the opposite. Servicing the flock may be a pleasant occupation, but it doesn't call for any great distinction in character; any second-rate billy goat can do it. It's commitment that calls for fierceness and vigilance and all the other qualities that make us think of the wolf as noble."

A reluctantly single woman friend said to me: "After a while, skipping from person to person becomes boring, because you're just doing the same thing over and over again. Pretty soon, you start to get it down, you do all the preliminary things without any ragged edges that somebody could grab and hold onto. You start getting so glib about your emotions that they lose their intimacy value, there's no feeling left. . . .

"When you make a stand with one person, you get to go on to other more meaningful things. . . . When you're married and something's wrong between you and your spouse, you can't just stomp out and call a cab. You have to deal with it. You have to scream, cry and argue and admit you were wrong—all those crazy, terrible things. There's something real about marriage and having to work around all these complications. It feels grown-up."

Laurie Colwin wrote in a short story published in the *New Yorker:* "Marriage was as deep as a well, as rich as the Bayeux tapestry, and with as many stitches and as much detail. Married people suffered and rejoiced over and over and over and over again. Marriage was a trench dug by time, a straight furrow, the mighty oak that has grown from a tiny acorn. Lovers were, by comparison, little scratches in the ground."

To become intimate, to change, to grow into a couple: These achievements are part of a process that requires time. The glory of marriage is that it provides both a reason and an environment for the adventure of becoming a better human being.

EIGHT

The Staying Power of Commitment

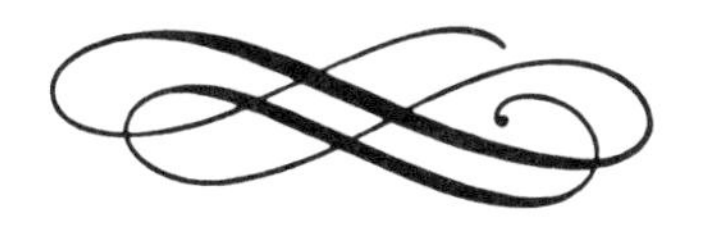

A WOMAN I KNOW SOMEtimes claims she envies me because I have an intimate relationship with someone I love. Although she's no fan of marriage, she says she wishes she had someone to love, and someone to love her.

I'm not so sure she really does. My friend may *think* she wants what I have, but what she really wants and generally manages to get is not love, but *to be in love.*

Being in love is the high-voltage, circuit-blowing infatuation we've all experienced when we connect with someone new. It's the intoxication of being accepted and desired. It's the thrill of taking a leap, shedding clothes and inhibitions, being dazzled by the private magnificence of another. Being in love is awesome and enthralling, but in the end, sadly, it's an emotional sprint. Like a flower it simply doesn't last.

Love, by contrast, is a marathon of the heart. It

requires training, discipline, endurance and work. It is not a spectator sport or an event whose outcome can be decided in seconds. It is pushing up hills and suffering pain, resisting the temptation to drop out. While love has its highs, they are generally more calming than electrifying—the satisfactions of simply being able, of persevering, of making progress toward a distant and significant goal.

Love, writes Erich Fromm in *The Art of Loving*, "is a 'standing in,' not a 'falling for.' . . . To love somebody is not just a strong feeling—it is a decision, it is a judgment, it is a promise. If love were only a feeling, there would be no basis for the promise to love each other forever. A feeling comes and it may go."

One reason so many relationships and marriages founder these days is that people too often confuse love and being in love. When the newness wears off, when the passion cools, when fights occur and problems arise, they immediately assume love has died and begin plotting ways to bail out with a minimum of carnage. What has really happened, of course, is that they're no longer *in* love, though they may be at a point where, if they're willing to make the effort, they can now begin *to love.*

Those who insist that their lives must constantly

crackle with the electricity of being in love, and who never advance to the more serene, sophisticated pleasures of love, inevitably begin believing that all relationships, including marriage, are inherently doomed, that they sprout, bloom and wither, that they have a finite life cycle that rarely coincides with the human life span.

When love is viewed as an act of will, however, it can survive as long as your heart beats. Put another way, while being in love may sometimes lead to marriage, it's love that makes a marriage last. More specifically, it's the deliberate, active commitment of love that is the core of conjugal bliss.

Commitment is essential to marriage because marriage is difficult. To begin with, marriage is not a truly natural state. In fact, while monogamy is common in nearly all species of birds, it is rare, as a rule, among mammals—the group of animals that includes us. On the other hand, human beings seem to have a deep, almost instinctive yearning for companionship, structure and security.

"There is an intrinsic and inescapable conflict in marriage," writes Jessie Bernard in *The Future of Marriage.* "Human beings want incompatible things. They want to eat their cake and have it too. They want excitement and adventure. They also want safety and security. These desiderata are difficult to combine in one relationship. Without a commitment, one has freedom but not security; with a commitment, one has security but little freedom."

Marriage today is more demanding than ever. With women asserting their right to be treated as equals, with both husbands and wives working at careers and simultaneously trying to raise children, with the media bombarding couples with the latest psychobabble about sex and the ideal marriage, with so many temptations and so little social support for such archaic virtues as fidelity, with men and women expecting so much from marriage, it is amazing that many marriages are as sound as they are.

"Marriage was once a harbour from which some marriages set sail safely, some lay in it and rotted, some were simply wrecked on the shore," observes Margaret Mead in *Male and Female.* "It is now a voyage in the open sea, with no harbour at any point, and each partner is committed to vigilance and deep concern if the ship is to sail at all."

Bookstore self-help sections are loaded with guides to success in marriage, and all of us are familiar with the qualities that lubricate a relationship We know about honesty, patience, loyalty, kindness, humor, communication and sensitivity. But what the marriage commitment demands above all is plain, old-fashioned hard work.

"The secret to making a marriage work can be

summed up in two words: enormous energy," said a friend recently reconciled with his wife. "When you have two professional people working ten or eleven hours a day, you come home and your body and mind are calling out to have the plug pulled, either by sitting in front of *Monday Night Football* or disappearing into a nice quiet corner with an escapist novel. If you let this happen often enough, it becomes a habit. Sooner or later, all your energies are devoted to working and recovering from work, and you end up without any strong, exciting emotional exchanges with your spouse.

"To do that can be a real time bomb. You're often not conscious of how bad it is. At some point, you have to come to the realization that your marriage is at least as important as your job or your efforts to recover from your job. To make it work, you have to save an awful lot of physical and emotional energy for your relationship. It's not something you can wait to let happen on its own."

Succeeding at marriage requires plenty of work, but so does any worthwhile accomplishment. "Marriage is but life in miniature," Havelock Ellis writes in *Psychology of Sex*. If married life "were all easy and pleasant, it would be but a feeble image of the world and would fail to yield the deepest satisfaction that the world can give to those who have drunk deeply of life. . . . Marriage as a creative personal relationship is *an achievement* between mates . . . often a very slow achievement."

The way to that achievement is littered with snares and barriers, and no one makes it without sweat and tears, bruises and scars, without boredom, frustration and rage. "I don't think it's possible to not get bored and wear each other down," a friend told me. "You have to believe in the value of the institution because you do get to a point where it becomes easier to part than to stay together. You have to have faith that your love is still there even when you don't feel it. That's what marriage is all about. If you don't get married, you don't build an edifice around the relationship that keeps it intact during phases like that."

The love that sustains marriage is, as Joyce Colony pointed out, writing in the *New York Times,* "the staying on *in spite of* . . . the acknowledgment that 'for better or worse' *includes* worse, something the old marriage has learned it must abide." Most veteran couples "have seen the breaking point many times and simply moved through it full throttle, like an airplane on takeoff. Perhaps feeling that too much hope and energy have been expended to turn back, they have rolled on toward the possibility that what they did not like would change and what they enjoyed would get even better."

There are times when a marriage is hopeless and the bonds should be broken for the health and future happiness of both partners. But for most people this is such a drastic and traumatic step that it is taken only as a last resort. Hence, one of the virtues of marriage is that it discourages precipitous action during periods of friction and disenchantment. There is a sense, when you get married, that you're in it for the duration. You tend to work harder at solving the problems, putting out the fires, guarding the perimeters.

Married love, writes Nathaniel Branden in *The Psychology of Romantic Love,* is "the ability to know that we can love our partner deeply and nonetheless know moments of feeling enraged, bored, alienated, and that the validity and value of our relationship is not to be judged by moment-to-moment, day-to-day, or even week-to-week fluctuations in feeling. There is a fundamental equanimity, an equanimity born of the knowledge that we have a history with our partner, we have a context, and we do not drop that context under the pressure of immediate vicissitudes. We remember. We retain the ability to see the whole picture. We do not reduce our partner to his or her last bit of behavior and define him or her by means of it."

In the end, then, married love may be simply a matter of attitude. A friend who's been married for fifteen years says staying married means being able—and most of all, willing—to fall in and out of love repeatedly with the same person. Several years ago, following a pregnancy, his wife gained a lot of weight. "When my wife became obese, it was one of the greatest disappointments of my life," he said, "and for several years, I was quite depressed about it. Then, one night a few years ago, we were on vacation and my wife was sleeping next to me. I woke up for some reason and looked over at her and began thinking about how much we'd been through together. Suddenly, I realized that I really *liked* her. After that, her obesity didn't bother me so much."

My friend's wife has slimmed down recently, and as he put it, smiling triumphantly, "I got back the girl I married." He is glad he had faith and that he stuck to his commitment. "When you live with someone for a long time, with a positive attitude, a special bond develops that becomes very durable. You're friends but also more than friends. In most successful marriages, there are times when 'spouseicide' is contemplated, but after a while, you learn to roll with the punches. I think it all boils down to approaching life with a sense of the joy of winning rather than the fear of losing. You have to look at what you might gain rather than what you might lose."

NINE

Buddy Love

IN HER BOOK *TALKING Woman*, journalist Shana Alexander, pondering her parents' fifty-year marriage, marvels, "They are a miracle, nearly extinct. My mother and father are the snow leopards of the social contract. I cannot know why they did it, how they survived it."

Sad to say, in today's moral climate, a long-lasting, happy marriage sometimes seems like a unicorn. We've all heard of it, and we all know what it's supposed to look like, but none of us has actually seen one.

I'm exaggerating, of course. Most of us have had the privilege from time to time of knowing married couples who truly seem to delight in each other, even after decades of matrimony. These are the blessed husbands and wives who still touch and fondle like lovestruck teenagers. They are the couples who still devour each other with their eyes at dinner parties. They are the ones who pine when they're apart and rejoice when they're together again. Over the years, they have become genuine friends of each other's enthusiasms, as fond of each other's follies and foibles as they are proud of each other's virtues and victories. Their marriages seem so strong that, to paraphrase the Talmud, they could sleep together on the blade of a sword. Indeed, one can't imagine them apart.

How pleasant, for example, to learn of the happy marriage of Harry Truman and his beloved wife Bess. For nearly fifty years, stretching from his days as a Missouri farmboy to his days as a retired President, Truman showered Bess with letters, sometimes two in one day. In so doing, he loved her, *Washington Post* columnist Colman McCarthy noted, "by the simplest and deepest ardency of all—paying attention."

Then there is the marriage of writer E. B. White and his late wife Katharine. When they were both working at the *New Yorker*, they frequently exchanged billets-doux through the office mail. In one memo, after asking his wife to change a couple of words in a piece, White signed off: "And thanks for unforgettable nights I never can replace."

And what a treat to read in *Time* magazine of the fabulous twenty-five-year marriage of Paul Newman and Joanne Woodward: "A few years ago, when he was filming in Hawaii, Paul handed Joanne a box with a new evening gown in it. When she had changed, they were flown to a deserted golf course where they were served an elegant dinner alone beside the sea, serenaded by a string quartet. . . . When Paul is traveling, he calls Joanne every day, and when they are in Westport, he will break off a conversation to say, 'I want to see my lady.' " On Newman's desk, he keeps an oval-shaped, sepia-toned framed picture of his wife as a teenager, looking demure and holding a rose. Under the picture, in fine gold lettering, it reads, PEOPLE I LIKE TO GO TO BED WITH.

Romantic? Yes. Rare? Yes. Impossible? No.

"There are a fortunate few who do have marriages where the bonding is so good that you get almost a physical sense of how close they are," says Sally Green, of the Marriage Council of Philadelphia. "These are marriages where there is real fusion—not the sick fusion of helplessly dependent people— but the kind of fusion in which $1 + 1 = 3$. These are people who are complete in themselves but who also have a relationship that is synergistic. Paradoxically, at the same time they've become united with their spouse in marriage, they've also become more of who each of them is. In other words, she is more she, he is more he, and as a couple, they transmit messages of vitality, belief, caring and values. In some cases, these couples can actually begin to look like each other. They begin using the same facial expressions and adopting each other's mannerisms and gestures."

In such marriages, so much time has gone by, so much perspective has been reached, that the couple realizes in a very visceral way: We're together, we're going to make it. And they breathe a sigh of relief. It is the moment when a husband and wife have coped with so much, when they have come to know each other so deeply, that there is finally real trust, the kind of pure, unalloyed, instinctive trust that exists between a newborn and a mother. It doesn't happen often, because achieving this trust takes time. There has to be a certain amount of experience together so that there can be predictability and security. There must be a certain amount of successful getting through, which the couple duly records and takes pride in, so that eventually the marriage itself emerges as a kind of lifetime accomplishment that they wish fiercely to protect.

For couples intent on reaching this state, the crucial factor seems to be nothing more mysterious than time—time for the marriage to mature to the point where both spouses appreciate the importance of waiting, of sticking things out. "Marriage," says a friend who has been married for eleven years to his childhood sweetheart, "teaches you patience. It gives you a sense of weathering the storm. The first few years are the toughest. There's so much you have to get used to. You're always clashing and banging into each other. But the longer you're married, the easier it is.

"My wife and I are very different in many ways. I like to go out; she doesn't. I'm athletic; she isn't. I like to drink; she doesn't. But over the years, we've grown closer. Maybe it's just from being together so much. The process is so subtle that I have a hard time describing it. It's just a feeling I have in my gut that we belong together, that there's been a kind of continental drift towards each other.

"Now it's hard to imagine life without my wife. She's responsible for giving me a lot of faith in myself. And the more I'm with her the more I learn to appreciate her. She's the most generous person I've ever met. She does things for other people without any inhibition or consideration of what she'll get back. I idealize her for the purity of her giving. Selfishly, I know if I became suddenly handicapped, she'd be there. She would still love me, and whatever we've got would continue."

Sociologists and psychologists have fancy, polysyllabic terms to describe the kind of bonding that occurs in good, long-lasting marriages. One that comes to mind is "companionate love." But I like the term my wife Tanya came up with one night when we were discussing changes in the quality of our marriage. At the time, she was somewhat bewildered because she missed the passionate intensity that characterized our relationship when we first fell in love, those euphoric days when we spent every second together and couldn't keep our hands off each other. She knew she still loved me, she said, perhaps more deeply and possessively than ever before, but it was not the same kind of love. "We're still lovers," Tanya said. "But now, we're more than that. We're best friends. We're buddies." Indeed, our marriage had evolved from "giddy love," the blind rapture of new-found lovers and honeymooners, to "buddy love," the quiet, assured fusion of road-tested, knowing companions.

As I look at my married friends, those who seem to have the sturdiest marriages are buddies with their spouses. "Romance isn't the subject of marriage," says one. "That's not what makes it work. It's not part of its everyday character. What marriage really does is provide you with a wonderful companion who you can laugh with and do things with and enjoy spending time with. That's not the stuff of romance, but it's not reasonable to expect to be romantic all the time. What life is all about is getting through the day-to-day stuff. In a good marriage, you have someone to help you get through it, and someone you can help get through it."

I had a conversation recently with the wife of a

colleague who is battling terminal cancer. She and her husband have a happy marriage that seems to have grown even stronger and closer despite the sometimes overwhelming worries and pressures they've faced since her husband's disease was diagnosed. Instead of cracking, they've closed ranks. Instead of surrendering to despair, they've affirmed life. Significantly, in the midst of this crisis, they conceived what will be their third child.

Reflecting on her marriage, this woman said, "Whatever happens, I know I've had something very special, something that very few people have. I have really loved somebody and been loved by somebody. I've gone through all the sorrow and joys associated with that. It's not been a crush, or a flash, but an ongoing process, a process that's changed me and made me a better person, a process of oneness, of becoming one person. It's corny but it's true. You go deeper and deeper into each other until there are no secrets left, no illusions, nothing but respect for each other's frailty and dignity. You keep tunneling into each other, stripping away the layers like an artichoke, until you get to the very core of trust and honesty."

What does it feel like there? I would describe it as a feeling of profound well-being, a feeling of elemental rightness and naturalness, a prelapsarian state of grace where both partners know each other so well that there are no inhibitions, fears or secrets. It's a feeling, wrote Barbara Lazear Ascher in the "Hers" column of the *New York Times,* "of total peace and security. Like finding yourself under a tropical sun in February, or listening to Stern and Rose play Brahms's 'Double Concerto,' or having your newborn, still connected by a cord, stare straight into your eyes." For those fortunate enough to attain this state, there is no road-to-Damascus revelation. Instead, there are a million small gestures and meaningful moments—a wise smile, a shared laugh, a soulful touch—that buttress the conviction that you have someone you can count on, someone who will listen and care and be there to laugh and cry, to celebrate and mourn.

Buddy love does not, of course, preclude moments of great sexual passion. Generally, in fact, couples who achieve buddy love also enjoy good sex. "You know each other so well that everything you do in bed is done right," said a married male friend. "Your body anticipates it. There's none of the awkwardness of sex with someone new."

"There comes a point in most relationships where the passion disappears," another male friend said. "It doesn't mean that sex gets boring. It just means that because of the depth of your intimacy, it becomes more transcendent. Like many triumphs and tragedies, sex is one of those things that demands to be shared with someone in a way that just plain friends aren't capable of."

By now, it should be obvious that buddy love cannot survive without trust and commitment. "If you enter into a pure unison," wrote D. H. Lawrence in *Women in Love,* "it is irrevocable, and it is never pure till it is irrevocable. And when it is irrevocable, it is one way, like the path of a star." Or, to put it another way, if trust is buddy love's food, adultery is its poison, for to be unfaithful is to nullify a relationship predicated on faith. Show me an "open" marriage and I'll show you a marriage based on deceit—overt deceit, covert deceit, deceit by commission, deceit by omission. In the final analysis, it amounts to this: Infidelity is no way to treat a buddy.

"Infidelity is no fair," writes Barbara Ascher. "Somebody is left out. Somebody else is having all the fun. . . . In infidelity, someone is the outsider. Being an outsider hurts. . . . I question those who say of their 'unsuspecting' spouses, 'He (or she) will never find out.' 'It had nothing to do with you.' That's like a pickpocket leaving behind a note saying, 'Nothing personal.' It may not be personal, but all the same you've been robbed. You've been had."

Those who've been married long enough to

achieve buddy love are generally also wise enough not to be inveigled by the transitory thrill of an adulterous fling. "When you've had sex with the same person for ten years, it's hard to sustain the level of excitement you felt in the first six months," said a married male friend. "There are times when I lust for other women, but I know intellectually that it would destroy my marriage and everything I really cherish. I also realize that no matter how exciting and illicit sex with someone else might feel right now, I'll feel like I'm married to that person a year from now. So for a few months' fling, I'd be jeopardizing a relationship that's been built up over a decade."

A reporter friend of mine who's been married for many years told me: "There are a whole lot of single women at the newspaper who are attractive and nice and who, if I wasn't married, I'd be interested in. If my wife died, there'd be lots of women I'd seek out, and eventually I'd probably marry one. But right now, none is competition for my wife. There's a great Paul Newman line. I'm not sure I've got the quote exactly, but once, when he was asked how he—a movie superstar and sex symbol—had managed to stay married to the same woman for so long, he supposedly said, 'Why go after hamburger when you've already got steak?'

"When I was younger, I wanted to be one of the 'boys on the bus'—one of those reporters who travels around the country following a presidential candidate. Several years ago, I did it for several months, and it was not what I'd thought it would be. It meant lots of lonely, boring nights in sterile hotel rooms, eating bagels on the run, and the guys I was working with were no better off than I was. I was glad I did it, because it was a good experience. But I've done it now, and it's behind me. To me, it's a lot like being single. I find nothing attractive about being single now, and I'd have to be stupid to do anything that would screw up my marriage. The grass is greener right here, with my wife."

A friend of mine who considers his marriage happy and who did have an affair says the experience taught him that "sex within marriage is really important; sex outside marriage is not that important." When the affair was winding down, he took a trip overseas to play in a tennis tournament. "While I was there, I began having these delicious sexual fantasies—not about my lover but about my wife. I came home full of desire for her, and I still regard her as the most appealing woman I've ever known.

"I still love to look at other women, but you reach a point where you find yourself asking, 'Is an affair worth the hassle?' When you were a kid, you'd kill for a piece of ass, but now you think, 'I'll get home too late. I'll be tired. Oh, who cares?' An affair runs out of steam; it exists only as long as you're willing to sustain the fantasy. It feeds on itself until it burns itself out. But a marriage is something to nurture and watch grow."

Although sexual exclusivity seems to be a necessity of buddy love, buddy love rarely thrives when one or both partners is clinging, suffocating and overly dependent. In the healthiest marriages, both partners are already complete in themselves. There is room for individuality, a respectful acceptance of differences, and enough openness so the marriage can be ventilated and enriched by stimulating people, activities and ideas.

In *Women in Love,* D. H. Lawrence addressed the importance of maintaining one's individuality in marriage when he defined the ideal marital relationship as "a conjunction, where man had being and woman had being, two pure beings, each constituting the freedom of the other, balancing each other like two poles of one force, like two angels . . . two single beings constellated together like two stars."

I like what a psychiatrist once told writer Susan Edmiston, who reported the words in a column in the *New York Times,* "A good relationship is like a good ski binding. It holds you tight enough but not too tight. It represents a compromise between holding you and releasing you so no permanent damage is done. Like a ski binding, a relationship also requires periodic adjustment to reflect the terrain, the state of the art and your skill in skiing."

The best marriages are between men and women who respect and cherish each other's individuality. To be sure, there is plenty of giving in, sacrificing and changing, but there is no surrendering of the essential self. These marriages are not mergers but joint ventures. When these couples are apart, they are sad; when they are together again, they are glad. But they are not Siamese twins, so interconnected and interdependent that they are incapable of functioning and existing alone.

Of course, a relationship in which there is too much space can be just as disastrous as one in which there is too little. As with most friendships, it is shared experience that cements the bond, and it is through kindness, thoughtfulness and understanding that buddy love flourishes. As Eliza Doolittle, the heroine of *My Fair Lady,* demanded, "Don't talk of love, show me!" Countless times, my blue moods on Monday mornings have been brightened by cards from my wife that say simply "I love you" or "I'm thinking of you." Often, during the day, she'll call me just to say hello. Many times, she has returned from quick trips to the grocery store with bags of my favorite junk food or cartons of my favorite ice cream. Sometimes, she'll just give me a new book or a new tie or a new pair of running shorts for no other reason than that she saw them and thought I'd enjoy them.

A couple of years ago, I was wearing a sweatsuit for my running workouts that was so tattered that my wife began pleading with me to throw it away. I resisted for a long time because the sweatsuit was one I'd worn since I was on the track team at Princeton, and it had great sentimental meaning to me. I also thought that most of the sweatsuits available in sporting goods stores were too flimsy and tacky.

Undaunted, Tanya made several calls to Princeton's athletic department and managed ("I practically had to sell my body," she laughed later) to obtain an official heavy-duty Princeton sweatsuit, with my alma mater's initials emblazoned across the chest. She presented it to me at Christmas, and when I opened the package and saw it, I was so touched by her thoughtfulness—evidence of her love for me and what I hold dear—that I not only discarded my old sweatsuit but began instantly to cherish the new one, which reminds me of Tanya and her goodness every time I wear it.

Recently, I learned of a similar tale of marital kindness—this one involving David McCullough, author and social historian. When McCullough's first book was published—a book he'd spent years researching and writing—he and his wife Rosalee celebrated with a publication party. "At the height of the party, Rosalee stopped everything and called everybody together," McCullough recalls. "She had a present to give me. It was a beautifully wrapped package. I tore off the wrapping and inside was a package of copy paper—yellow copy paper. She said, 'This is for the next one.' She was really saying, 'We've been through hell to produce this one, but go ahead, don't stop now.' "

While thoughtful surprises make buddy love blossom, it's often the private rituals of affection that keep buddy love alive as the years go by. Listen to this moving testimony from a married woman who wrote me not long ago to tell me of the birth of her second child—and the long, loving marriage of her grandparents:

> My grandfather was a man who was not afraid of being sentimental, not afraid of showing he cared. He and my grandmother always were very tender with and thoughtful of each other—little things counted. They especially liked to give each other cards—"greeting" cards I guess they're called—on holidays, anniversaries, etc. And they made an art of finding the "perfect" card. My grandmother usually addressed Grandpa's cards quite properly, "To Fred," or some-

times "To Dear Fred." Invariably, she signed them "Love, Me." My grandfather always addressed his cards to her "To My Dahling"—and signed them according to whimsy or whatever secret joke they were sharing at the time.

My grandmother died 10 years ago, a thin, gray, shrunken little woman who, at the end, couldn't even talk. The only time she'd brighten was when Grandpa called to her, saying (with his unconquerable Boston accent), "Hello, Dahling." She was heartbreakingly senile—breath-holding frail—and had been so for 10 declining years. Grandpa took care of her, alone, all that time because, he said, he knew that she would have done this for him.

When Grandpa died last year, we (my father, mother and I) had to go through his things, his house. (He'd maintained the retirement home he and Grandma built outside of New Haven.) It was hard being in the house without him, hard to open drawers, etc. Hardest of all was finding in his bedroom closet neatly stacked and labeled boxes of cards—cards he and Grandma had exchanged. I started to go through one box—it began, I think, in the late 50s, early 60s—and found that as the years progressed and Grandma failed, Grandpa had started to give himself cards from Grandma. Probably, in the beginning of her decline, he'd done this to prevent her embarrassment at having forgotten. Later, I suppose, it was symbolic—a homage to the past, or something. And long after she'd gotten to the point where she couldn't even smile at the bright Easter bunnies or sunny birthday flowers, Grandpa continued to address the cards "To My Dahling" and to decorate the envelopes with the drawings the entire family had, over the years, come to love and expect.

That box I opened contained something more than cards—and that's why my mother took it back to Pennsylvania, and tied it up neatly, to save it all. . . .

Anyway, I feel lucky to have been a part of a family who values marriage—or is it partnership? My parents have a very happy, loving marriage/friendship/partnership too.

So I believe it can happen.

Amen.

TEN

A Personal Creed

From time to time, I like to watch moronic movies—flicks of the James Bond–Burt Reynolds genre, packed with girls and guffaws; Tanya won't spend a nickel on a film unless it's subtitled in French and deals with the Meaning of Life. I like to scale mountains, to canoe rapids, to take physical risks; Tanya buckles seatbelts, locks doors and worries constantly that I'll kill myself doing something "foolish." I like to go out and about once in a while, to see new faces and meet new people; Tanya's idea of a perfect evening is to cuddle up next to a crackling fire with a compelling book, a glass of wine, and just me. I have a tendency to be a "people-pleaser," engaging all sorts of folks in casual conversation; Tanya abhors small talk and calls me a "face man" because I'm so "promiscuously nice." When I'm writing or working on a project around the house, I keep at it until it's perfect; Tanya claims I'm a "neurotic" and that I waste precious time on stuff that doesn't really matter. I have a lot of willpower and self-discipline; Tanya has been known to consume a whole pint of ice cream or a package of cookies in a single sitting. I'm always late and I usually dress like someone who shops at the Salvation Army; Tanya takes pains to be punctual and wear clothes that are both proper and stylish. I'm a hopeless Pollyanna, always looking for rainbows in the middle of downpours; Tanya is an incorrigible doomsayer, able to conjure up worst-case scenarios for every stroke of fortune. I like to do things spontaneously, to "play it by ear"; Tanya is a planner who wants everything nailed down months in advance.

And yet, in spite of all these differences—actually, because of them—we love each other. Riding together back and forth to work, we have wonderful times telling stories and laughing or commiserating about the craziness of our jobs and the characters we have to cope with. Throughout the day, Tanya is always calling me or sending me notes. When work's over, I love to see her face. We still jog together in the park. We still hold hands in the movies. We still flirt with each other in public. She still drives me mad with desire.

I enjoy being a married man. I like wearing a ring and I'm proud of what it says about me and what I stand for. For the first time in several years, I feel good about myself. Free from the distractions, preoccupations and insecurities of singlehood, I can direct my energies elsewhere, concentrating on endeavors of lasting value and significance, such as making a home and creating a family. These days, my life feels in sync again, my soul feels whole again. The sunshine has returned to my smile.

Is this just the ecstasy of a newlywed, the zeal of a born-again husband? I don't believe so. Rather, it's the result of living in a way that accords with my philosophy of life. My religious background makes me a walking embodiment of ecumenicism. I was baptized a Catholic, confirmed an Episcopalian, married the first time by a Methodist minister, and at various intervals while growing up, I attended Presbyterian and Quaker services.

Nevertheless, the great moral principle that guides my life is not a line from Scripture but a line from a novel. "A sense of the fundamental decencies is parcelled out unequally at birth," wrote F. Scott Fitzgerald on the opening page of *The Great Gatsby.* For me, that phrase—"a sense of the fundamental decencies"—sums up the lessons of the Ten Commandments, Jesus' Sermon on the Mount, St. Paul's epistles, and the Golden Rule. For me, it means to be unselfish and giving, to be polite and kind, to respect and care for others, to make a contribution, and, if possible, to leave the world a better place.

Because of my belief in this principle, I also believe in marriage. For marriage, it seems to me, encourages the fundamental decencies. It provides an institutional setting that fosters unselfishness and giving, politeness and kindness, respect and care for others. In short, it enables human beings to become more humane. Furthermore, I believe, a good marriage is the best environment in which to raise children, the future of society and the world.

By contrast, the singles scene is a mean, Darwinian jungle. In the absence of etiquette, convention and tradition, the only rules are brutal: use or be used, screw or get screwed. Predators and exploiters thrive, and a kind of undeclared guerilla war rages on, with otherwise decent people raiding the weak and vulnerable for quick sex, a quick ego stroke, a warm body to get them through the night, or the winter, or the present crisis of spirit.

Obviously, not all married people are noble. There are plenty of married scoundrels and plenty of horrible marriages. Certainly, marriage has no magical power to make fundamentally indecent people suddenly decent. But for people of goodwill and sincere intentions, marriage offers not only a safe harbor and a bulwark against the world's woes but also a private sanctuary where you have more than a fighting chance to become your very best.

ELEVEN

The Story of a Good Marriage

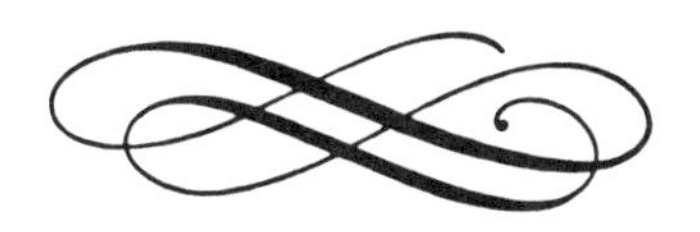

As I mentioned earlier, my parents did not have a happy marriage. Indeed, if my attitude toward marriage had been shaped solely by memories of my parents' relationship, it's highly unlikely I'd be married today. Fortunately, while growing up, I knew, and spent a great deal of time with, two people whose marriage was good: Edward and Elizabeth Norris Lynch, my grandparents.

They met in 1918, introduced by a mutual friend. By outward appearances, they made an improbable couple: he, the lusty, cinematically handsome, banjo-strumming son of a Shakespeare-quoting Brooklyn cop; she, the refined, convent-reared, harp-playing daughter of a proper Philadelphia lawyer who always wore a vest and a high starched collar.

They courted for three years, strolling around town, riding horses and playing tennis in Philadelphia's Fairmount Park, going to the movies ("Would you care for some refreshment, Miss Norris?" my grandfather asked his wife-to-be after they'd seen their first silent film together). At one point, they spent a chaperoned week at Pocono Manor Inn, an elegant Quaker-run resort in the Pocono Mountains of Pennsylvania. During World War I, when my grandfather was serving as a submarine listener aboard a navy destroyer, my grandmother, then a chief yeomanette at the Philadelphia navy yard, bolstered his morale by sending him letters and "care" packages of cakes and cookies.

On June 8, 1921, my grandfather and grandmother were married at St. Francis De Sales Roman Catholic Church in West Philadelphia. They honeymooned at the Lake Mohonk Mountain House in the Catskill Mountains of New York State. A full week cost them only $105. In my grandfather's study, mounted and framed, is the Philadelphia Trust Company check drawn to pay that bill, as well as the resort hotel's dinner menu and congratulatory wedding telegrams from friends. Surrounding these souvenirs are scores of photographs that, along with three bulging family photo albums, chronicle the many happy times my grandparents shared: Sunday drives in a sporty 1916 Mercer; family picnics in Fairmount and Valley Forge parks; outings to hear the bands of John Philip Sousa and Victor Herbert; splendid Sunday night dinners on the roof of Philadelphia's Bellevue Stratford Hotel; trips to the Catskills, Washington, Williamsburg, Quebec, Vancouver and Alaska, vacations in Maine and Ocean City, New Jersey; boisterous cookouts and parties at the family mansion on the Main Line; and throughout, the fresh, exuberant faces of their four children—a fey, angelic-looking son, and three cover-girl-gorgeous daughters.

But there were also tough times. During the Depression, my grandfather's business shrank to almost nothing. One year, his income was only $600. To keep his family fed and clothed, he borrowed from relatives, moonlighted as a bill collector and wrote screenplays at a picnic table in Fairmount Park. Later, two vacation homes—one in Maine, the other in Ocean City—burned to the ground, incinerating the dreams that went with them. Worst of all, there were the troubled lives and untimely deaths in their thirties, forties, and fifties of all four children—successive, staggering blows that wounded my grandparents to the quick.

In weathering these crises, my grandparents had many disagreements and quarrels, but no matter how disgruntled they got or how much they sulked, they remained committed and loyal to each other. They never stopped treating each other with respect and courtesy, and when they were feeling well and times were good, their affection for each other was obvious.

My grandfather, an expert amateur chef, was always whipping up exotic desserts to please my grandmother's finicky palate, and whenever my grandmother would chide him in front of the family for some endearing excess, she'd always conclude by reminding us, "I've been lucky to know two good men in my life, my father and your grandfather." At other times, clutching my arm, she'd say, "Your grandfather has been very good to me. Promise me you'll take good care of him after I'm gone."

About ten years ago, my grandmother fell and fractured her pelvis. Her health was soon under attack on several fronts: a weak heart, crippling arthritis, asthma, emphysema, a peptic ulcer and glaucoma. By 1981, when she was nearly eighty-seven, she could barely lift her head. Her legs were constantly swollen and she could no longer walk. Breathing was so difficult that it was a feat for her to complete a sentence. She refused to go to a nursing home, and my grandfather, who knew it would kill her, refused to let her. Instead, he insisted on becoming her full-time nurse.

He prepared all her meals and gave her medication more than twenty times a day. He pushed her wheelchair, and helped her bathe and brush her teeth. He lifted her into and out of bed and on and off the toilet. He sorted out her pills, and gave her eye drops and nose drops. When she gasped for air, he sprayed an inhaler into her mouth or held an oxygen mask over her face. The duties were endless and consumed all his energies from the time he awoke till the time he fell asleep. Every five minutes, it seemed, my grandmother was summoning him. And always, he responded swiftly, cheerfully. His selflessness, his ability to give and to love, put me to shame. At the same time, I marveled at how joyous he was, even though I knew that his insides were being gored by grief.

As my grandmother's mind began failing, she became unreasonably petulant, scolding my grandfather for trivial offenses. But he just smiled and laughed and redoubled his kindness toward her. When my grandmother began telling the same stories over and over again, he never let on. He listened attentively, as if he were hearing the tale for the first time, and he always chuckled at the same stale punch lines. On Sunday, without fail, he pulled out his prayer book and he and my grandmother said Mass together.

By the early summer of 1981, my grandmother was a wraith. Her flesh had shriveled away. Her skin was transparent and tissue-like. Her hands were gnarls of veins and bones. And her eyes—hollow, sunken, practically blind and eerily wide—gave her an astonished look, as though she were appalled at what had become of her or had already glimpsed the answers to the final questions.

At night now, in a feeble, doleful monotone, she began calling my grandfather. "Ed . . . Ed . . . Ed," she would repeat. The chant echoed faintly through the darkness like some haunting, otherworldly mantra, as though my grandmother had already passed on and were begging my grandfather to join her. Hearing it, he would rise out of bed and go to her side. He would smooth her wild white hair, then sit in a chair next to her and hold her hand and stroke her arm. He would do this, sometimes for hours, until she fell asleep. Then he would try to steal back to bed. But often, as soon as he began drifting off, she'd awake, and the chant would resume: "Ed . . . Ed . . . Ed . . . Ed . . . Ed."

As the summer wore on, my grandmother stopped calling at night, and my grandfather then knew she was about to die. He was right. On August 13, 1981, she was unusually serene and cooperative. Despite the great pain she was suffering, she managed to smile several times. That evening, as my brother David was dressing her bedsore, she suddenly said, referring to my grandfather, "Where's Daddy?"

"He's in the other room. He'll be right back," my brother said.

My grandmother paused, seeming to reflect.

"I love Daddy," she said.

Those were her last words. She breathed her final tortured breath a few minutes later. My grandmother and grandfather had been married on earth for sixty years and sixty-six days.

The day after my grandmother died, my grandfather suffered a back pain so severe he could barely stand up. He had strained his back a few days before while trying to hoist my grandmother from an awkward position. Now, suddenly, this man with the proud military posture, this remarkably robust athlete who was still lifting weights and playing squash, tennis and golf at eighty-four, was almost a cripple. The physical injury was real, but I couldn't help thinking that the pain in my grandfather's back was acute heartache.

In time, my grandfather's back healed, and so did his spirits. Being the kind of man he is, he mourned privately for the most part, though occasionally I caught him with red and sodden eyes. He began sitting at a different place at the dining room table so he wouldn't have to look directly at my grandmother's empty chair. He left her room just as it was when she passed away, except that over her bed he hung her art school diploma and a scholarship certificate, as though he were expecting my grandmother to return home for the holidays after her first semester at college.

He removed an oil painting from the living room and replaced it with my grandmother's wedding picture. So now, as he read in his rocker, all he had to do was glance up and he could see her as she was on June 8, 1921, so virginal and innocent, her mouth caught in a coy half-smile, her hazel eyes beguilingly impish. He began playing his Victor Herbert album more and more, the one with the sweet, sentimental melodies he and his wife liked so much when they were young—"Kiss Me Again," "Gypsy Love Song," "Ah, Sweet Mystery of Life" and "For I'm Falling in Love With Someone." And over the big upholstered chair where my grandmother spent so many hours, my grandfather hung this framed bit of verse:

Fifty years seem very long
But these fifty have swiftly gone
With less of tears and more of smiles
Fifty happy sunny miles
Happier years because of you
Brave and tender, kind and true
May the years ahead stretch far and wide
With us and happiness side by side

To Betty from Eddie
June 8, 1921–1971
(The above paraphrased from a jingle you composed and sent me in 1936 marking fifteen years.)
Christmas 1971

Several months after my grandmother died, I asked my grandfather about his marriage. It was late at night and we were sitting in the living room after dinner. His marriage had been happy, he told me, and he had never broken his wedding vow nor been seriously tempted to. He told me that he prays to his wife often and that he feels she is very close by. Sometimes, he said, he can hear her call him.

"We're still bound together, just separated physically," he said. "Someday, I expect to be rejoined with her."

"But isn't there a part of you that's relieved that Grandma's dead?" I asked. "Taking care of her around the clock was such an incredible burden on you. I don't know how you put up with it. Aren't you glad that's over?"

"Artie, with all her incapacities and all that that involved, I'd give anything to see her there now," my grandfather replied, nodding toward my grandmother's favorite chair. "God, what I wouldn't give."

SOURCES

Alexander, Shana. *Talking Woman,* Delacorte: New York, 1976.

Ascher, Barbara Lazear. "Infidelity Means an Outsider, Hurting," "Hers" column, the *New York Times,* February 24, 1983.

Banashek, Mary-Ellen. "A Good Man Is Still Hard to Find," *Mademoiselle,* January, 1978.

Bane, Mary Jo. *Here to Stay,* Basic Books: New York, 1976.

Berger, Brigitte and Peter L. *The War Over the Family,* Anchor Press/Doubleday: New York, 1983.

Bernard, Jessie. *The Future of Marriage,* Yale University Press: New Haven, 1982.

Branden, Nathaniel. *The Psychology of Romantic Love,* Bantam: New York, 1981.

Calvert, Catherine. "Why Aren't All These Nice Men Married Yet?" *Mademoiselle,* December, 1978.

Cantwell, Mary. "The Appeal of the Heel: Why Women Fall for Stinkers," *Mademoiselle*, July, 1979.

Colony, Joyce. "What Keeps Some Marriages Going?," "Hers" Column, the *New York Times*, September 23, 1982.

Colwin, Laurie. "Swan Song," the *New Yorker*, April 18, 1983.

Davidson, Sara. *Real Property*, Pocket: New York, 1981.

Doudna, Christine, and Fern McBride. "Where Are the Men for the Women at the Top?" *Savvy*, February, 1980.

Edmiston, Susan. "Building a Universe on the Basis of a Man's Slim Remark," "Hers" column, the *New York Times*, August 5, 1982.

Eisenberg, Lee. "Looking for a Wife," *Esquire*, December, 1980.

Ellis, Havelock. *Psychology of Sex*, Harcourt Brace Jovanovich: New York, 1978.

Fromm, Erich. *The Art of Loving*, Bantam: New York, 1963.

Furstenberg, Frank F., Jr. "Conjugal Succession: Reentering Marriage after Divorce," University of Pennsylvania, Philadelphia, 1982.

Hammer, Signe. "Why Nice Guys Finish Last With Women," *Mademoiselle*, July, 1979.

Jones, Landon Y. *Great Expectations: America and the Baby Boom Generation*, Ballantine: New York, 1980.

Kleiman, Dena. "Many Young Women Now Say They'd Pick Family Over Career," the *New York Times*, December 28, 1980.

Langone, John. *Like, Love, Lust*, Avon: New York, 1980.

Lasch, Christopher. *The Culture of Narcissism*, Warner: New York, 1979.

Lawrence, D.H. *Women in Love*, Bantam: New York, 1969.

Leonard, George. "The End of Sex," *Esquire*, December, 1982.

Mailer, Norman. *The Prisoner of Sex*, Little, Brown: Boston, 1971.

May, Rollo. *Freedom and Destiny*, Norton: New York, 1981.

Mead, Margaret. *Male and Female*, Dell: New York, 1968.

Millett, Kate. *Sexual Politics*, Ballantine: New York, 1969.

Murphy, Mary. "The New Celibacy . . . Yet Another Surprise Spin in the Sexual Revolution," *Los Angeles*, August, 1980.

Novak, William. "Are Good Jewish Men a Vanishing Breed?" *Moment*, January/February, 1980.

Novak, William. "Manhunt," *California Living*, the *Los Angeles Herald*, August 14, 1983.

Rothman, Stanley, and S. Robert Lichter. "Media and Business Elites: Two Classes in Conflict," *The Public Interest*, Fall 1982.

Sellers, Pat. "Couples," *US* magazine, November 9, 1982.

Shames, Laurence. "The Eyes of Fear," "Ethics" column, *Esquire*, September, 1982.

Shames, Laurence. "Wolves Mate for Life," "Ethics" column, *Esquire*, November, 1982.

Skow, John. "Verdict on a Superstar," *Time*, December 6, 1982.

Updike, John. *Couples*, Fawcett: New York, 1968.

Wolfe, Linda. *The Cosmo Report*, Arbor House: New York, 1981.

Wolfe, Tom. *In Our Time*, Farrar, Straus & Giroux: New York, 1980.

Yankelovich, Daniel. *New Rules: Searching for Self-Fulfillment in a World Turned Upside Down*, Bantam: New York, 1982.